What's On Your Mind?
How to Defend Your Faith and Stay Friends

By Jeff Greer

Published by Bright House Publishers, LLC
3040 East 38th Street
Anderson, IN 46013

Copyright © 2018 Jeff Greer

All rights reserved.

No part of this book may be reproduced, stored in a retrieval system, or transmitted by any means, electronic, mechanical, photocopying, recording, or otherwise without the prior written permission of the publisher.

Distributed by IngramSpark

For ordering information, please contact Bright Corp. at 1-800-428-6424

Library of Congress Publishing-in-Catalog

    Greer, Jeff.
        What's On Your Mind
        ISBN: 978-0-692-117750 (ebook)

            1. RELIGION/Christian Life/Devotion
            2. RELIGION/Christian Life/Inspirational
            3. RELIGION/Christian Life/Spiritual Growth

Printed in the United States of America

Table of Contents

Acknowledgments 4
1/ Smiley Faces 5
2/The real question: Why? 11
   More from Jeff 35
3/Why does God allow suffering? 37
   More from Jeff 56
4/Who determines right & wrong? 57
   More from Jeff 72
5/Atrocities in the name of God 77
   More from Jeff 89
6/Can you prove God? 92
   More from Jeff 100
7/Pure luck or divine intervention? 103
   More from Jeff 114
8/Still Smiling 116
   More from Jeff 118
Some final thoughts 119
Notes 121
Resources 123
   What's the Truth about the Crusades? 126
   Science Increasingly Makes the Case for God 132
   Suggestions for Further Study 135
   Glossary 138

Acknowledgments

I CAN close my eyes and remember so clearly the first time I heard Ravi Zacharias speak. I was sitting in a classroom at Nyack College in 1981, preparing myself for a long lecture from Professor C. I was waiting for him to pull out his yellowing three-by-five cards and start reading the same material he had used for the past 30 years (though I did love him). As I stretched my fingers, preparing for marathon note-taking, in walked a very distinguished gentleman. He said in his classic voice, "My name is Ravi Zacharias, and I'll be teaching your class this morning."

For the rest of the class I was mesmerized. His words were concise, his stories were captivating, and he closed his eyes when he quoted Malcolm Muggeridge and C.S. Lewis as though he was worshiping God through his lecture. I must have looked like a fool, sitting in the back row of the class with my jaw hanging open, wondering how anyone could speak with such inspirational intellect. I don't think I took one note that day. I didn't want to miss what he was saying because he never wasted a word. When class was over I stayed behind so I could talk to this man who had opened my eyes to the world of apologetics and motivated me to learn. When I finally had my chance, I walked up to this intellectual giant of the faith and said something profound: "How did you get so smart?" He smiled and with a kind and humble spirit he responded, "Through years of study."

I tell that story because this book would not exist without the tireless effort, passion and conviction of men like Ravi Zacharias. When I first heard Ravi speak at Nyack I had only been a Christian for a year. Since that time, I have read his books, listened to him preach, and had the opportunity to speak with him many times through the years. I would love to think that I have a few original thoughts in my response to my friend Emily (who you will meet in this book), but most of them come from years of studying and applying the arguments and responses of Ravi and others like him. Thank you, Ravi, for discipling so many of us when you may not have known that you were. Thank you for setting an example with your life and through your words that others can follow. And thank you for inspiring me to learn.

1/ Smiley Faces

WHEN I was a teenager, no one really knew what to do with me. I had very little ambition, no real talents or special abilities to speak of—just a whole lot of anger.

My parents divorced when I was eight, and I lived with my mother while my brother Mark lived with my father. From first grade through sixth grade I had moved nearly every year. The experience of being in a new school, each year feeling like I was on the outside looking in, only fueled my frustration. I became a very cautious, distrusting person. I spent more time defending myself as the new kid and playing catch-up in school than I did building friendships and learning. The constant changes began to wear on my emotions.

From sixth grade through high school I grew up in an apartment complex in New York. Only one of the kids in that complex had a father who lived in their home, and no one talked about their family situation. Your feelings were your own, and they stayed trapped inside.

As time passed, fear turned to anger and hopelessness. I began drinking. I drank for one reason—to drown my intense feelings. I didn't want to have a good time; I wanted to numb myself.

During my junior and senior years in high school, my anger was becoming more intense and my drinking only seemed to increase my negative feelings.

By my senior year my emotions were out of control. I used to say my philosophy of life was, "I hate everyone I don't know, and I hate most people I do know." The fights I had avoided for years I now began to seek out. I had to unload my anger on someone or something. So I punched holes in walls, kicked doors off their hinges, and increased the drinking that I used to drown my feelings. My emotions were at a breaking point.

Then an old friend, Patti, invited me to a church youth group meeting in someone's home. To be honest, I thought she must be in a cult or something, because she was too happy. She smiled too much. I told my friend Don that we needed to find out about this cult so we could get her out of there.

So my first church experience was going to someone's home. When Don and I arrived I was amazed to find a group of high school students singing and smiling and talking openly about God. I was used to being in groups where hostility reigned—starting with insults and ending in a fight. This experience was totally different for me.

But my amazement was overshadowed by my ingrained mistrust of people and of any new environment, and this one was no exception. After I walked into the house I made my way to the top of the stairs where I could keep everyone and everything in front of me. I didn't trust anyone to be behind me.

As I was sitting there watching and listening at the top of the stairs with my friend Don, the youth pastor brought out some Play-doh. Play-doh? You've got to be kidding. "Make something that reminds you of a special time you spent with someone in this group," the youth pastor told us.

What had I gotten myself into? Where I lived no one played with Play-doh—far from it. Don and I wanted to leave. But I had put myself at the top of the stairs, with no one behind me and everyone in front of me. The last thing I wanted to do was go through all those people and draw attention to myself. I was trapped.

I said to Don, "Here's the plan. I'll make something for you, you make something for me, and we'll never talk about this again." I quickly molded a football and gave it to Don; he made me a ball and bat. We sat there for a few minutes plotting our next move, when something profound happened.

Two girls from the group, Patti and Emily, approached us, balancing a large piece of cardboard covered with Play-doh shapes. On each bright circle were pressed tiny Play-doh features to make a smiley face. There were 30 or 40 of them. Emily presented them to me and said, "We're all glad you're here."

As I took the gift from the girls, I tried to look cool. But on the inside my hard, skeptical heart began to change. As I look back, it seems as though God reached down and put both his hands around my heart—he knew exactly what it would take to get through to me. The mistrust and insecurities that had kept me apart from God all my life, that had trapped me at the top of those stairs, were the very thing that God used to reach me.

I still have a few of those smiley faces; they're over 35 years old. Those smiley faces are the reason I went back to church the second time. They're not the reason I believe in God, but they did open my heart to the possibility that there was a God, and that life could be different.

Fast-forward thirty years. I'm sitting at home one evening with my computer, and I open my Facebook page.

You have a new friend request.

 **Emily**

 **Jeff Greer**
May 6

How are you? I hope all is going well. I think about our old group all the time. I would love to get everyone together some day. You may not remember this, but you were the one who made me the smiley faces out of Play-doh the first time I came to youth group. You may not know it, but that had such an impact on my life. I still have a few of them. It's what caused me to come back. Simple acts can have amazing results.

Check out http://www.grace-chapel.com, http://back2back.org, http://www.innovatespectra.com, http://www.sseinc.org, and realize that a smile can change the world.

Have a blessed day. Hope to hear from you soon.

Emily
May 6

Hey Jeff! So great to see you, and MY GOODNESS, all you've been up to. What a busy and full life you have. Your wife must be amazing! Ha!

So funny what you wrote about the Play-doh faces. I remember when you and Don first came to youth group. What a profound decision it was for you to stay: Don found his wife, and you found your life's work. A smiley face is very valuable indeed. I'm so proud of all you've done! Wonderful, wonderful. I wish I had your ambition!

Thirty years and I can see that our lives are remarkably different. We're opposite! (But that's not bad—opposites are good for defining who we are.) You are a minister, and I am a <u>nullifidian</u> happily raising my three kids without any religion whatever. Imagine that. Does that surprise you? Recently, someone told me that I was a bad parent because I didn't bring my kids to church. So that made me not smiley, but sad. And a little angry. The person who said that was mean and thoughtless, but you knew that.

I am married to Mr. Wonderful: does laundry, brings home bacon, puts up with my dreams and schemes. I have three fabulous children: boy, boy, girl—14, 12, 10. They love music. Playing it, singing it, listening, writing, everything is music. All of it makes me smile, broadly.

I've worked as an artist and writer for 25 years in the publishing biz. All good. I don't paint enough. Or finish what I start. Me thinks you finish what you start. (I have vision overload too! Once a dreamer, always a dreamer.)

Let's plan on staying in touch. I need your help remembering those happy play-doughy days.

nullifidian: a person who has no faith or religion

Jeff Greer
May 7

Emily, it's so good to hear from you. My daughter Jen leads worship at our church. Kim, my oldest, is married and working in the youth ministry. They are both very talented. Deb and I started Grace Chapel in 2000. We have a ten-year-old son we adopted from Mexico. He's the best. We are going to travel the world together fighting injustice. I have a passion to help orphans and widows.

I think the person who said you're a bad parent doesn't read their Bible enough. They may just be religious—that means nothing.

I would love to hear why you are no longer walking with Christ. Maybe I'm wrong, but I think people sometimes walk away from the faith because they don't see Christians living out what they say they believe. I believe what God promises, and I have lived, seen and experienced things that most people can only dream about. I hope we can talk. I would love to hear your thoughts and share mine with you. I'm so glad to hear you're married and happy with your family and life. Say hi to them all and keep smiling.

Emily
May 7

I love that you and your family want to travel the world and fight injustice. Hooray! You're a superhero!

So, since you asked, I have a lot to say about my spiritual journey. I agree with you about why people walk away from faith. But there are other reasons too. For me, it's been more philosophical than evidential. While there are great memories from my time in faith— and I wouldn't trade them for anything—I came to realize that I was there for the social, not the spiritual. A harsh reality that I never really fully embraced until years and tears later.

In my heart, I always knew that faith did not ring true for me. But it was my secret. I lived a guilty lie for a long time. I was the great pretender. But I was just convinced that my square peg had a home somewhere. So I struggled, looked for churches, prayed. I thought I could repackage the words or ideas to make them easier to swallow. A different religion, a different book, a different minister. Until one day, sitting at a <u>Unitarian</u> church, I had this great epiphany: I have the choice NOT to believe. And, like that, I saw my square peg for what it was—just a piece of wood that I could carve into any shape I wanted.

I literally cried tears of joy for the liberation. Like taking a step off the edge of a cliff and then coming to this great realization that I can fly! I have not an ounce of regret. I feel like my brain and my heart are aligned now and I have clarity. I also have a tremendous thirst for knowledge which I think was missing when I was walking among the faithful. In fact, I feel like faith and curiosity are often at odds.

I ADORE the subject of faith and religion. I majored in philosophy at college and never stopped studying. I take classes, and go to seminars, and read until the wee hours; I have a mile-high stack of books on religion and history. One of my favorite authors is Dale McGowan who writes about secular parenting. I also love the work of Bill Bryson, Timothy Ferris, Brian Greene and <u>Sam Harris</u>. Just read a great book called "Misquoting Jesus" by Bart Ehrman. I like to read about the fabric of the universe, and how/why we believe, and about the history of faith and customs. It's all so exciting to me—can't get enough!

Feel free to write and share your thoughts.

Unitarian: a liberal denomination that believes God is one being, rejecting the doctrine of the Trinity.

Sam Harris: a critic of religion and considered the father of "New Atheism."

2/ The real question: why?

Jeff Greer

May 8

Thanks so much for taking the time to explain your journey. I would love to talk sometime. I want to send you a book that I just read. It's a response to Sam Harris's book *A Letter to a Christian Nation*. I think where I get stuck is when I think of life without God. Even before I was a Christian I struggled with it. Here are my thoughts . . .

If God is taken out of the discussion, life becomes meaningless. The great questions of the universe become meaningless. Why ask them? What is the purpose of questions—or my life, for that matter? Without God there is no right and wrong, no good and evil. Terms become meaningless and using them hypocritical. If I say something is good, then I assume that there is evil; if there is good and evil then there must be a moral law that determines what is good and evil, right and wrong. If there is a moral law then there must be a moral law giver—God. Without God the concepts of right and wrong are meaningless, so why use them? Without God suffering, love, truth and knowledge are also meaningless. For people to remember past abuse with no purpose in their suffering is a cosmic nightmare. Without God humanity's only value is what we create in our own finite minds.

> **moral law:** the rules of behavior a group of people follow out of conscience and that are not necessarily part of written law

If I were not a Christian I would be a nihilist. Nihilism looks at a world without God and comes to a logical conclusion: Without God life is meaningless and any thought to the contrary is a delusion of the mind (not my words, but theirs). I'm a very black-and-white thinker. I deal with suffering every day, so it's very difficult to see these truths only from a philosophical framework without the practical implication.

I love having these conversations. I hope I'm not coming off too "preachy." Please share your thoughts.

God bless, Jeff

Emily

May 9

So, Jeff, it sounds as though you ARE a nihilist! At least in the way that Nietzsche used the term. You state it plainly: there is no meaning in life; words have no meaning; suffering, love, have no meaning; there is no right and wrong, and no sense even in questioning—WITHOUT God. So the stated problem of no meaning is solved with the alternate, more satisfying concept of God. Your nihilism bolsters your faith: "It couldn't be this bad thing, so it must be that good thing."

Jeff Greer

May 9

I'm not sure it's "this" over "that," but what's the truth. I consider myself a seeker of truth. When I started going to church I asked a lot of questions, seeking truth. I don't want to believe in something that's not true; I don't care how it makes me feel. God for me is not an alternative to a less satisfying worldview; God just makes more logical and rational sense. For example, I think it takes more faith to

> **nihilist:** a person who believes that truth and values are baseless, and life has no meaning or purpose

be an <u>atheist</u> than it does to be a Christian. A Christian starts with a first cause for existence, God. An atheist starts with nothing and believes by faith that nothing created everything, which is impossible according to his own worldview. It is a leap of faith that is beyond my own. So it's really not "it couldn't be this bad thing, so it must be that good thing." It's just that one worldview is more reasonable.

Emily

May 10

You say you are a truth seeker. That indeed is the $64,000 question. (BTW, that was up to the million dollar question a few months ago, but with the economy it's back to 64K!) Mankind has been asking that same question since the beginning of time itself. But what is the criterion for assessing the Truth? Is it <u>empirical</u>? That is, determining the what, how and why of reality with some sort of predictability which approaches the ultimate Truth? If so, I would suggest science is the proper tool. If by Truth you mean determining the <u>metaphysical</u> nature of life, including its cause, and purpose, then perhaps reasoning and <u>semantics</u> are the road to take. Personally, I am inspired by the writings of <u>Immanuel Kant</u> who suggested that both empiricism and reasoning fall short in determining Truth (or reality).

Regarding his belief in god, he was like: "Well, we can't really know, and we can't really conclude, but believing doesn't hurt anyone and

---

atheist: a person who believes there is no God or supreme being

empirical: based on experiment and observation rather than theory

metaphysical: concerned with abstract thought or subjects, such as existence, causality, or truth.

semantics: the study of the relationship between words or symbols and what they mean

Immanuel Kant: an 18th-century German philosopher who believed that the world is unknowable and morals are based on human reasoning. Considered the father of modern philosophy.

in fact can actually help people, so no harm done." Of course that's a huge paraphrase, but you get the idea.

My question for you is: As a born-again Christian, haven't you already concluded that God *is* truth, or at least gives meaning to truth? Is God the spectacles that help you SEE the truth? I think I'm just too fascinated with the detail and mind-boggling nature of scientific discovery to wear those glasses.

Jeff Greer

May 10

Emily, yes, I do believe that God is truth. And I do see truth from God's perspective. But I don't believe that stops me from enjoying the excitement of discovery. I love trying to understand the mysteries of the universe. You seem to see God as a limitation to discovery, and I don't understand why. Science and God are not always at odds and when they are, it's usually based not on the desire for truth, but on a political or philosophical agenda.

One thing I have learned is that people are not just influenced to believe or disbelieve because of the evidence. The issue of belief has as much to do with the heart as with the head. Charles Darwin came to his disbelief in God after the death of his daughter Annie. After she died his belief in a moral universe ended, and with it his faith. This period was said to chime the final death-knell for his Christianity. It was the evil/suffering question that led Antony Flew

---

born-again Christian: someone who has repented of his or her sins and turned to Christ to be saved from spiritual death

Charles Darwin: English naturalist who formulated the theory of evolution by natural selection

moral universe: a basically spiritual universe that is ordered by a higher power and influenced by good and evil

Antony Flew: a philosopher who was an atheist most of his life but later came to believe in God based on scientific evidence

down the same path, a path that he changed later in life. I have found while reading atheists that it is rarely the intellect alone that leads them to disbelief; experience plays a very powerful role.

I believe that most people decide their beliefs and then spend their lives trying to prove them. Well, to be honest, most people don't have the courage to give it much thought; they scream in their minds, "Don't confuse me with the evidence." If you believe in the miracle of evolution, you will find evidence to back it up. I'm not attacking the scientific community; all I'm saying is that they are just people.

What I love about the Christian faith is that it challenges you to think, to reason, to seek truth—because in the end all truth leads to God.

When we try to understand the universe and its complexity, we all ask questions concerning the meaning of life. The "what" and "how" questions can be researched through science, but it's the "why" question that is at the heart of humanity. Stephen Hawking summed it up when he said, "Now if we only knew why, we would have the mind of God." The "what" gives us the stuff of existence, but it's the "why" that gives us the larger understanding of our existence. Would you agree that it's only as we come to an understanding of the "why" of life that the "what" of life becomes defined and meaningful?

Polanyi in his book *Meaning* argues that our society gives science its meaning rather than science giving meaning or truth to society. He says that if science is misapplied it can destroy life rather than contribute to it. He believes that religion, poetry and art are the disciplines that give life meaning and purpose, not science.

Science has its place in seeking truth, but it falls short in answering life's most profound questions. The whys of life silence the scientific voice and leave the philosophical mind at a loss. If you don't answer

> **evolution:** genetic change passed on from generation to generation by such processes as mutation, natural selection, and genetic drift. Here, it is used to mean development of one species into a different species.
>
> **Stephen Hawking:** A physicist, cosmologist, and author, widely known for his groundbreaking work while having a severe physical disability

the "why" question, seeking knowledge becomes a meaningless intellectual exercise.

I admit that God is my foundation, and some would say that decision limits my ability to seek truth, or squelches my curiosity; but I would say that without a foundation it's hard to build anything, including a worldview. And knowing that there's a God gives purpose to my curiosity. I want to understand the hows, and the whats, and the whys. I want to know all the complexities of the universe, and what's at the bottom of the ocean, and the mysteries of humanity. But it's my understanding of God that gives meaning to my search.

Emily

May 12

Regarding God and science: It's common to reference the quote by Hawking, and also Einstein's "God does not play dice" to buttress the argument for god. Two things here: First, I mentioned earlier that I think a scientific discussion about the existence of God is futile. Using names or quotes by famous scientists does not make for a scientific discussion. There are as many (or more) quotes by the same scientists and many others that would state the contrary. For example, Hawking also said: "Why does the universe bother to exist? If you like, you can define God to be the answer to that question." It is nothing more than a verbal maneuver: God = the unexplained beginning of the universe. Nothing is gained by switching one concept for the other. They both still have to be accepted on FAITH. Or not.

Secondly, and most importantly, is the inexplicable LEAP that the cause of the universe, no matter what you call it, is an omnipotent, omniscient, omnibenevolent personal Creator. All humankind's good

> **omnipotent:** all-powerful
> **omniscient:** all-knowing
> **omnibenevolent:** all-good

traits on steroids, and none of the bad. It's very tidy.

Here's the rub: For those of us who are on the outside of the box, all the "stuff" that comes from this tidy solution feels contrived, and frankly, some of the details are devilish indeed. Never mind about the intellectual contortions (virgin births, infanticide, cruel and unusual punishment). The hardest part to swallow is that when you run into a genuine philosophical stumbling block, the answer is always MORE FAITH.

At the very least, I see <u>dogma</u> as a limitation to understanding: the dismissal of Darwin's theory being the prime example.

Jeff Greer

May 13

I get the feeling that you think if you believe in God you have to check your intellect, creativity, curiosity, etc., at the door. I know that those in the church can often be lazy and don't like challenging questions, but God says, "Come let us reason together." I have a lot of questions, but I don't see that as inconsistent with my faith. I see it as a part of my faith journey.

Please understand that Christians don't "dismiss" Darwin's theory, they simply disagree. If Jesus is who he said he was and if man is created in the image of God, then Darwin cannot be right. Either Jesus was telling the truth or Darwin's theory is true. It's the law of non-contradiction: a truth's opposite cannot also be true. Either you're created in the image of God, or you're here by luck or chance. To a Christian, Darwin's observations may be fascinating and worthy of discussion, but he is mistaken in his final conclusion.

Why is this important? Because if mankind evolved, then we have no value outside of what others choose to give us or what we give ourselves. Why is that significant? Emily, you are a kind person, but

> **dogma:** an official system of principles and beliefs, especially in a church

there are those in this world who are not. What was the bloodiest century in the history of the world? The twentieth. Hitler, Stalin, etc. followed a naturalistic worldview to its logical conclusion.

Ravi Zacharias [*The Real Face of Atheism*] writes:

> In his book *Modern Times,* the historian Paul Johnson referred to Hitler, Stalin, and Mussolini as the devils of the 20th century. Interestingly, Nietzschean dogma influenced each of them. So profound and operative was Nietzsche's philosophy upon Hitler it provided the conceptual framework for his onslaught to obliterate the weak and inferior of this world. That being done, Hitler would establish the supremacy of the "superman" in an unobstructed and dominant role. Hitler also personally presented a copy of Nietzsche's work to Mussolini and Stalin.

Nazi mastermind Adolf Eichmann's last words were to refuse repentance and deny belief in God.

> I understand that these arguments don't make evolution wrong. All I am saying is that you must follow your worldview to its logical conclusion. No God—no human value—and with it the consequences.

Good-hearted people can try to give others value and purpose, but those people are few and they fall short. The best the world can offer is "live and let live"—until the culture changes its mind and decides that some people are inferior in some way, and decides to get rid of them.

True atheists like Voltaire and Nietzsche were honest and consistent

---

naturalistic worldview: the belief that nature is the only reality, and it can be understood through experience, reason, and science

Ravi Zacharias: a philosopher, author, and speaker who presents logical defense for Christian beliefs and principles

Voltaire: an 18th-century French philosopher who was highly critical of religion

Frederich Nietzsche: a 19th-century German philosopher who denounced religion, rejected Christian values, and advocated nihilism.

in their worldview. They admitted that without God everything is pointless and life itself is ridiculous. The idea that you have any meaning or purpose to your life is, in their words, a delusion of your mind. People are just random mutations, and if you believe differently, you've just deluded yourself so you can live in the real world. Nietzsche actually predicted that the twentieth century would be the bloodiest. How could he make that prediction—and be right? Because he understood the implications of a worldview without God. If people have no value, then it makes no difference whether or not someone like Hitler or Stalin puts people in a gas chamber.

My worldview tells me people have value because they are created in the image of God and therefore deserve my respect, my love, my compassion and, if necessary, my life to save theirs—weak or strong, friend or enemy. Jesus tells me I must consider others better than myself; that I should look to their interests, not just my own. He tells me the weak are not inferior, but need to be protected and cherished.

Emily

May 13

I find value in everything—with or without god. I think good and evil, right and wrong are simply adjectives that describe something's quality. It's intrinsically subjective and most often it is culturally defined. Considering your travels and your work, I assume you see this firsthand: What you and I would consider reprehensible is tolerated in some cultures.

Jeff Greer

May 14

I have a hard time placing "value" on something when value is defined in strictly human terms. When right and wrong become subjective they lose all meaning. I want to seek the truth. But even truth becomes subjective if I follow this line of reasoning. So truth, right, wrong, evil, good all become subjective. They only have value in the mind of the individual. If that's their only significance, who cares? I think that's why nihilists call this thinking a delusion of the mind.

Emily

May 15

I do believe that we long for purpose, but why must that be defined by religion? Ayn Rand, who founded the philosophy of objectivism, believed that the greatest way to achieve purpose and meaning in life was through the creative process. I agree whole-heartedly. Not just artistic creation; it can be relationships, families, common goals. Life is so beautiful when we're fully engaged in those fleeting moments of creativity. And the best thing is that in the end we have a product to show for it!

One of my most favorite quotes is from Ben Franklin: "If you are not to be forgotten when you are dead and rotting, write something worth the reading, or do something worth the writing."

Why can't we draw meaning from our own experience and understanding? Why must it be part of a bigger plan? Someone else's bigger plan? Can't we simply appreciate art for art's sake, love for love's sake, life for life's sake? "Isn't it enough to see that the garden is beautiful, without having to believe that there are fairies at the bottom of it too?" [Douglas Adams]

Jeff Greer

May 15

I guess what I'm saying is that when we kill God we must create an alternative that helps us live in a meaningless world. Instead of God

> **Ayn Rand:** A Russian-born author and philosopher who developed Objectivism, a practical philosophy that rejects faith and religion. Politically, she supported individual rights in a capitalistic system.

giving definition to those terms, we become our own god. We tell ourselves that life has meaning because the alternative is incomprehensible. The human mind longs for purpose. It seeks knowledge and it desires to create, because we reflect our creator. I believe you are an outside-of-the-box thinker with a desire for truth, and I believe that this journey you are on will ultimately lead you back to the one who crafted you.

How about I just send you a smiley face? That should change your mind—it worked with me. ☺

Emily, if I ever say anything that offends you, please let me know. As we continue to talk that would never be my desire.

Emily
May 16

You are just the cutest thing with the smiley faces. Love it.

Offending me? Well, you're talking with someone who went to a state school, lived on a farm, gave birth to three kids, and ran the PTA for eight years. Impossible!! I really, really enjoy the conversation we're having and I hope you do too. Likewise, I hope I don't sound flip or disrespectful.

Perhaps you can use some of this as fodder for an upcoming sermon: "Conversations with a Happy Heathen."

Jeff Greer
May 16

I love talking about all of this as well. As for offending me—after 30 years in ministry I have very thick skin. Great sermon title, by the way. But I don't consider you a heathen, more of a pagan (just kidding). I think of you as a prodigal taking the long way home. Just keep in mind I'm known for being relentless when I care about

> **pagan:** a person who worships nature or the earth

something and as I write this I am looking at one of the smiley faces you made for me—do the math.

Emily

May 16

I would not be offended by being called a pagan, not in the least. But a pagan I am not. Self-identified pagans are, generally speaking, polytheistic—and I have a hard enough time believing in ONE god!

I would also definitely not qualify myself as an atheist. I agree with you that it takes a lot of faith (as much?) to denounce the existence of something as it does to believe. Atheism is too aggressive for my taste. I'm not interested in believing in a negative, or proclaiming that a person of faith is delusional or simply wrong. There is no benefit whatever in that point of view.

The existence, or non-existence, of God is a futile discussion. It's a matter of FAITH, not proof. So those who seek to prove or disprove based on some scientific calculation (like Dawkins, for example) play a fool's game. God exists because you believe that god exists. Period.

That reality compels nearly everything in your life. It's your passion, your inspiration, your life's (good) work. Who would seek to disparage that? Not me.

Jeff Greer

May 17

I don't think discussions about God are futile. The God question is for me the most important question that anyone can answer. I do agree it comes down to faith, but that should not stop one from searching

> **polytheistic:** believing in more than one god
>
> **Richard Dawkins:** a British biologist and atheist known for his criticism of creationism and intelligent design

for truth, because the implications of the question itself are so significant. I guess that's why it matters so much to me. I can't see any of this as just a philosophical or intellectual exercise, because every day I deal with real people asking me real questions. They want answers, not theories and empty jargon. This week a family lost their dad. Two teenage girls and their mom are now looking for someone to speak to their loss. Someone else lost their twin sister. I'm not God, and I don't have all the answers; but what do Darwin, Hawkins or Harris have to offer? "Sorry, what a shame. Better luck next time."

Ravi Zacharias was debating an atheist at a university when someone called in to ask a question. The woman on the line was very upset. "You say that there's a God," she said. "Well, if there's a God, then why does my child have cancer?" Ravi very quietly and respectfully said to her, "Madam, before I answer your question I would like to allow my opponent to answer first." Silence. The atheist just shrugged his shoulders. He had no answer—apart from God there *is* no answer. He was silent because he had nothing to offer.

Emily
May 17

Dear Jeff, Your writing today has really moved me. Your passion and thoughtfulness is very evident and you make so many good points. I'm so sorry to hear about the losses that you have had to help people through this week. It makes me feel guilty that I've taken any of your time with this philosophical debate when you are needed to hold these people up. I'm thinking of you and your congregation and hoping for peace in your hearts.

I think the anecdote about the silence from the atheist is interesting and telling. I would guess he (or she) would say if you don't have the answer, don't make something up!

It makes no difference to me whatever if a person believes or doesn't believe. As long as there is consideration, respect, honesty and no harm done, then I'm smiling. If belief is the thing that causes that sort of behavior, then yeah!

On the contrary, my non-believing self isn't depressed at all! In fact, I feel free and happy living in the present and it is my daily goal to truly appreciate all that I have: my wonderful healthy kids, my family and friends, the beautiful sunshiny day (today!), my freedom, my education, my literacy, etc. At our family dinners we say what you would call a prayer: "We are thankful for this food, for health and home and all things good, for wind and rain and sun above, but most of all for those we love."

Jeff Greer
May 19

Let me again try to speak from the depths of my heart. I cannot just enjoy life from the perspective of enjoying the here and now because that's all there is. Maybe I could if I were only concerned about myself—please don't take that as applying to you—I'm trying to look at the perspective, not the person. I cannot separate myself from the rest of humanity, and much of humanity is suffering. The idea of living in this world without purpose—that no matter how hard we try, true purpose and meaning cannot exist without God—is unimaginable for me. But that is not my main point here. If I just thought about life without God, that the how and why didn't matter, if being fully engaged in life was all that was important, I would lose my mind and my heart.

To watch the suffering and injustice of this world and think, "Well, that's their problem, too bad they weren't lucky enough to live in America, it's just survival of the fittest—the strong crush the weak, so be it." When I think of the world from just a <u>temporal</u> perspective it is—I can't find the words—it brings you happiness, it's your dream, but it's my nightmare. I can't live in a world where the strong run wild with no consequences. The only justice is what MAN decides it is. So people suffer here in this life and then they die. Others inflict the pain and they are happy and then die.

> **temporal:** concerned only with the present life or this world

I can't help but cry out like Habakkuk, "Why do you make me look at injustice? Why do you tolerate wrong?" [Hab. 1:3.] I cannot separate my life from reality. I ask the questions and find my answers in the eternal. When I see things only from a temporal perspective there are few answers, but when I see them from an eternal perspective I see this life as only a small part of our journey. Jesus taught this constantly. He engaged the afflicted, he touched the lepers, he showed compassion to prostitutes and he healed the sick. But more than that, he gave them hope for the future.

You seem to detest the idea of a future life. In America we don't seem to think much about it because this life for most of us is not too bad. I think you see a belief in an eternal future as something negative and controlling, but to those who are suppressed, afflicted, persecuted, treated unjustly or suffer in a multitude of ways, all they have is the future. Knowing that evil will not go unpunished and that eternal life waits for the righteous has given courage and hope to billions. It is not the bane of their existence; it brings them joy and peace.

Jesus lived and died to make sure that that hope was not just an empty promise but an absolute fact. How others choose to use that truth is a discussion for another day. When I think of a world without God, emotional freedom is the last thing that comes to mind. We all struggle with these difficult questions; the difference is when a hurting world comes to the atheist there is complete silence and only accusations.

I think G.K. Chesterton said it best: "When belief in God becomes difficult, the tendency is to turn away from Him; but it heaven's name to what?"

I know you share some of the same frustrations that I do; we are just looking through different lenses. I have never been able to see life from the perspective you do. There is a scene in the movie *Arthur* that may help you understand my feelings. Arthur is struggling with a decision, knowing how it will affect those around him. At one point

> **G.K. Chesterton:** an early 20th-century English author of hundreds of books, poems, essays, and stories

Lancelot looks at Arthur with frustration and says, "Arthur, you long for a world that will never be." I, too, long for a world that may never be, but I will fight with relentless passion until my dying breath to change it as much as I can, knowing that one day I will stand before Jesus and hear, "Well done, good and faithful servant."

 **Emily**

May 20

I don't think that people who are non-believers offer silence as an answer to suffering. I think there have been great non-believers who have done great things to alleviate suffering: Clara Barton is a good example. And yes, there are countless good deeds done by believers, too. But I would say it's not the belief in god that motivates them, but their humanity. If it is the former, (to avoid hell or gain heaven) then their deeds are good but the motivation is selfish.

I think the focus for the nonbeliever is not on the why. We don't know why some people suffer and others don't; it's a matter of luck, circumstance, good genes, or whatever. Does it really matter *why* when a house is on fire or the flood waters are rising? If you offer God as a reason for good OR evil it just creates more questions.

So I ask someone like you: Why can't WE be enough? Why can't WE comfort each other, help each other, rescue each other? Why can't we appreciate the great compassion, love, will, creativity, beauty of mankind without having to invent a superhuman sky fairy, with all the bells, whistles, books, rules, damnation, salvation, immaculate conceptions, transubstantiation, guilt, judgment, prayers, angels, demons, power, fear, *et al*?

Immaculate Conception: The Catholic doctrine that the Virgin Mary was conceived without any stain of original sin

transubstantiation: The Catholic belief that the bread and wine are changed into the body and blood of Jesus during Communion.

Jeff Greer
May 21

What I'm trying to explain is that's part of my problem. That was my problem as a non-believer. When faced with the unexplainable nothing there are no answers that satisfy or, often, even attempt to. If I'm suffering and ask for help, the response is "we don't know," "it just is," or "it doesn't matter." If nothing leaves us with nothing, it allows people to put the issue out of their minds. There is no moral obligation to respond, only what the individual deems necessary. (Am I missing something? If I am, please clarify.) My worldview will not allow me to put a difficult question out of my mind, and it was the question of suffering that led me to Christ.

The world is filled with suffering and cries out for answers. I'm not saying I have all the answers, but I need to respond based upon the knowledge and revelation I have. I must also do all I can to alleviate that suffering. I don't know how else to say it. Nothingness is empty. "I'm suffering, why?"...silence. For someone who has spent his life trying to help others, that silence offers a hopeless future both to the person helping and the person needing the help.

Just a side note, I do understand why that philosophy is so appealing to people. Entering into another person's suffering is sometimes difficult to bear. I understand why Jesus needed to be alone sometimes. It must have been overwhelming. Letting go of that responsibility on any level can seem very attractive. You (not you specifically) don't have to wake up at night thinking about what so-and-so is going through; you don't have to feel so intensely. You don't have to think of ways to overcome the odds or fight the next battle of injustice—and the next one and the next one.

Emily
May 22

You write: "If I'm suffering and ask for help the response is 'we don't know,' 'it just is,' or 'it doesn't matter.' If nothing leaves us with nothing it allows the individual to put the issue out of their minds. There is no moral obligation to respond, only what the individual deems necessary. (Am I missing something?)"

YES! YES!! You're missing something. You're jumbling two completely different things into one: Origin and Morality. For the origin question, we both end (or begin) with an unknown. As I understand it, you are dissatisfied with the unknown and have accepted God as the knowable "solution" to that problem. I, on the other hand, don't feel any compulsion whatever to fill in the gap. I am comfortable with the simple notion of "we don't know yet" or "it doesn't really matter" now.

This not knowing has no bearing whatsoever on whether or not we have a moral obligation to one another, or if we can determine a collective understanding of goodness, for example.

I don't say, "I don't know how the universe started so therefore I don't care if there's suffering." That's crazy.

I guess the flip of that is: "I can't bear that there is suffering in the world. There must be a reason for it, and therefore there must be a God." Some would say that's crazy.

Jeff Greer

May 23

No, I am not dissatisfied with the unknown and therefore see God as the solution. If I study and contemplate the unknown or nothing as my first cause it leads me to logical conclusions. As G.K. Chesterton puts it, "To believe in the nonexistence of God would be analogous to waking up some morning, looking in the mirror, and seeing nothing." Let me try to put this in another way. A person who says that God *cannot* exist is, to say the least, muddleheaded. To hold to the belief that there is no God the person would have to demonstrate infinite knowledge, which is tantamount to saying, "I have infinite knowledge that there is no being in existence with infinite knowledge." I can understand questioning God and searching for truth, but I struggle with a person who claims that <u>absolutes</u> do not exist and then makes absolute statements. Again I cry, "If you have a worldview, stick to it—follow all of it to its logical conclusions!" <u>New Atheists</u> want God not to exist, but then they want all that a Christian worldview has to offer: purpose, meaning, human value, morality.

So once I face those conclusions and find them wanting on so many levels, I continue to search for truth—and that truth leads me to one conclusion, that there is a God. Once I come to that conclusion I live within that worldview, and if I face difficult questions I search for truth until I find an answer.

I think we also have to agree to disagree (at this point) that you can have meaning and purpose in a "something-from-nothing" universe. I would strongly argue that the only purpose people with that view can have is that which they create in their own minds. Meaning is only what they want it to be. In a sense, they are the god of the world they create, and they find happiness living in that world. I don't think someone with that view is crazy, only wrong and a bit illogical.

Emily

May 26

I read an interesting opinion piece today by Dale McGowan, director of Foundation Beyond Belief, discussing the response of atheists to

> **absolute:** something that does not depend on anything else for its existence or for its specific nature (opposed to relative)
>
> **New Atheists:** a group of early 21st-century authors who share the central belief that there is no supernatural or divine reality; that religious belief is irrational and empirical science is the only or best source of knowledge; and that there is a universal and objective secular moral standard. This moral component and their more aggressive attacks on religion set them apart from Old Atheists.

the Virginia Tech shootings in 2007. He says that Dinesh D'Souza accused atheists of being absent in times of human suffering. "Notice something interesting about the aftermath of the Virginia Tech shootings?" D'Souza asked. "Atheists are nowhere to be found."

Needless to say, McGowan, being an atheist, found D'Souza's comment "not only profoundly mistaken but also deeply offensive." He then quotes an online post by an atheist professor at Virginia Tech who felt he should respond to D'Souza because "there is at least some vague sense amongst people that we atheists don't quite grasp the enormity of [the Virginia Tech] events, that we tend towards a cold-hearted manner of thinking, that we condescend to expressions of community, meaning, or bereavement." That professor participated in the very campus events meant to bring healing that D'Souza said were ignored by atheists.

"There were also surely atheists and humanists among the emergency responders and doctors and nurses and counselors who fought valiantly to stitch together shattered bodies, minds and hearts," McGowan says. "The atheists weren't absent. They were invisible. Their bodies and skills were easy enough to see, of course. But their convictions—that this is our one and only life, that its loss is something to fight hard against, that we have no one but each other to rely on when bad things happen—those convictions went unnoticed. Prayers and songs and religious rituals announce themselves. Quiet conviction goes unseen."

Jeff Greer
May 27

I believe that all people are created in the image of God. We all have the laws of God written on our hearts. I want to make one thing very clear. I think you are a kind and loving person. You love your family and friends and care about the feelings of others. True atheists can't

> **Dinesh D'Souza:** an Indian-American political commentator, author, and defender of Christian beliefs

live out their worldview, and if they tried they would be miserable and go mad. That is really not a knock, just a rational observation. We can debate these concepts and I will point out the flaws in the logic, but in the end I know everyone is created by God and has his nature stamped on their souls. I would be amazed if atheists on the Va. Tech Campus didn't care and did nothing. It would be unnatural. Not knowing what to say and not caring are two different things. Most atheists do not, nor do they want to follow their worldview to its logical conclusion. Theory and reality are two different things. We can debate but in the end we are all humans. Never question my respect and belief in you.

Emily
May 29

Full disclosure: I hate that you believe this: True atheists can't live out their worldview, and if they tried they would be miserable and go mad." That's just a ridiculous statement, judgmental, intolerant, naïve, and false.

I am a nonbeliever. I know plenty of nonbelievers. We are compassionate, loving and smart. We are good parents, and good citizens. We possess moral judgment. We don't MISS having belief. We don't WISH we had belief.

And we are not miserable or on the brink of madness.

Put the shoe on the other foot—if someone said that YOUR worldview leads to misery and madness, how would you feel?

Insulted? Defensive?

I feel I am compassionate and caring not in SPITE of my worldview, but BECAUSE of it. There is only one life. Here and now. This is why life is so incredibly, ineffably precious. It needs our care, defense, love and value here and now. That is my worldview.

"We can debate but in the end we are ALL HUMANS. Never question my respect and belief in"—YOU!

Jeff Greer

May 29

Boy, did that post backfire on me. I need to rethink what I was trying to say and try again. I need to go out, but I'll connect again tonight. Yes, you are loving and thoughtful, smart and compassionate. No argument. Boy, I ticked you off. I don't think you feel loved and respected. I'm very sorry.

Emily

May 29

OK. I'll accept and appreciate another try. ;-)

I look forward to your reply. And yes, I'm still smiling.

Jeff Greer

June 2

OK, let me try this again. This line of reasoning is meant to clarify my thoughts.

I believe that everyone is created in the image of God, even if they do not. My worldview tells me that because everyone is created in the image of God, they are capable of amazing acts of love and kindness. It is therefore not surprising to me that professing atheists on the Virginia Tech campus acted in loving and kind ways.

I see no purpose in attempting to make the claim that atheists on the Va. Tech campus did not act in loving and kind ways (as Dinesh D'Souza did) because it does not contradict my formally stated belief system.

They claim that they acted in loving and kind ways because they chose to, and it was not based upon any belief in God. I would assume such a claim because they are atheists, just as they would not be surprised by my assumption based on my beliefs.

Emily, we need to discuss the difference between Old Atheists and New Atheists. My comment about not being able to live out their worldview is based on the writings of more traditional atheists. Also, when I talk about atheists I don't assume I am talking about you; you do not claim to be an atheist.

When we state our positions we lay out what we believe to be true. You yourself said, "I cannot, and therefore will not, accept the idea of creation. It requires me to eliminate rationality, logic, evidence—just can't do that."

Do you really believe that I am irrational, illogical and have no evidence for what I believe? Where does that leave me? Your disbelief leads you to that conclusion. I understand that.

When I said, "True atheists can't live out their worldview and if they tried they would be miserable and go mad," I'm speaking of pure atheists who claim that any thought of life that does not lead to despair is a delusion of the mind. A life of despair is a life of misery.

You may not agree with my view of pure atheists, but I don't believe my statement was ridiculous, nor do I understand how it's judgmental, intolerant, naive or false.

Bottom line is, I want to be able to discuss these issues without being disrespectful to you. That is very important to me. Our worldviews conflict, but that just means we need to walk a bit lighter to avoid toe injury.

I don't agree with many of your views, but I respect you and do not question your intellect. You are my friend regardless of your

> **Old Atheists:** people who adhere to the traditional belief that there is no supreme being or beings, differing from 21st-century New Atheists who are openly antagonistic to religion and whose beliefs are typically based more in science than in philosophy

worldview, and I know you feel the same.

I hope this post does more good than harm. Let me know what you think. As if anything could stop that.

Emily
June 2

Old atheists, new atheists, old Christians, new Christians—labels, labels everywhere and not a drop to drink! LOL

More from Jeff

Is there meaning and value and purpose to life without God? When we're trying to understand what we believe, that question becomes foundational.

In his book, *Can Man live Without God?* Ravi Zacharias said, "There is at least one thing that both theists and antitheists agree on, and that is that no matter what the starting point, we must all attempt to answer the question of life's meaning."

What is the purpose of your life? What does it matter that you were born? These are life-defining questions, and each of us will have to decide what we believe—it's unavoidable.

I would submit to you that if you eliminate God from the equation, life has no meaning, your questions have no meaning, human value has no meaning, the deeper questions of the universe—all the things we like to talk about and think about—become meaningless. Why even ask those questions if you and I are here on this blue globe by mistake, by accident, by luck?

Apart from God people often allow their culture to define meaning for them—money, power, and fame seem to be high on the list. Others try to look within themselves for meaning, or define it in their own terms: I choose what meaning is, what purpose is—whatever works for me; whatever is right for me. Meaning becomes whatever I want it to be.

Lee Iacocca wrote in his book *Straight Talk*, "Here I am in the twilight years of my life, still wondering what it's all about...I can tell you this, fame and fortune is for the birds."

Without God, the foundation of your beliefs is up for grabs.

Intellectual discussions do not get to the heart of these intense longings and questions that people have about life and God. Most people ask questions not for debate, but for understanding. They are going through real experiences, real pain, and they want to understand why. It doesn't matter how they ask the question; they could be aggressive and obnoxious. But behind it all, most of the time, is a sincere person who is truly trying to understand the "whys" of their own life. They

> **theist:** someone who believes that one God created and rules the universe

want to know, and it's irresponsible of us as Christians not to try to give them the best answer we possibly can.

Each of us has a worldview, whether you realize it or not, and that worldview will have an effect on every area of your life. Consider: which worldview gets to the heart of the human longings we all experience—a naturalistic worldview or a Christian worldview?

3/ why does God allow suffering?

AFTER that first online interaction I thought about Emily and the divergent spiritual paths we had taken over the past thirty years. I thought about how we, as Christians, often share or defend our faith. We can forget that we are talking to unique people with different experiences who come to conclusions for different reasons. I remembered the words of C.S. Lewis, "Humans are very seldom either totally sincere or totally hypocritical. Their moods change, their motives are mixed, and they are often themselves quite mistaken as to what their motives are." Each of us faces challenges that cause us to walk down different roads looking for answers. In our politically charged culture it's so easy to attribute negative intent or motives to people's words rather than try to understand their feelings. When I thought about Emily, I didn't want to let cultural presuppositions about "how the other side thinks" influence our conversation. I just tried to remember my friend, a teenaged girl who had the courage to reach out to me at a time in my life when I really needed a simple act of kindness. I kept that in mind as we continued our conversation. Emily was not an adversary, but a friend I care about, someone loved and valued by God.

Emily

June 5

Here's the granddaddy of all questions: Why does ONE person's choice to "turn against God's love," as you call it, result in the pain and suffering of the innocent and godloving/godchoosing? Is it collateral damage? Does the fact that "some good comes of it" make it justified?

Christians seem to have a tidy answer to every question: It just takes more faith. Why does God allow suffering and evil? "Well, God has a plan and we just have to trust him!" It's the moral equivalent to being "sshh'ed." That response not only does not satisfy, it actually repels.

Jeff Greer

June 6

I agree that people need more than "God has a plan." Every day I deal with people suffering beyond what many can bear, and I can assure you the conversations go far beyond "God has a plan." But as I think about it, he does—though I do understand your point. I think you have spent too much time with the wrong Christians.

Every day I need to answer the questions of the universe: Why is there suffering, why do babies starve in Africa, why is there evil, why did my mom die, why am I dying, why did I lose my job, why can't I overcome this addiction, why don't my parents (my husband, my wife) love me . . . where is God? And every day I go to the source of my strength—the one who came and walked this earth, the one who understands our suffering because no one ever suffered more—and pray for the right answers. I need answers that will heal, bring peace, bring hope, and bring comfort.

The question of suffering and evil is a topic that is not only on the minds and hearts of those "outside of the box," as you call it, but within the church as well. I can understand your frustration with those who would give an incomplete answer to a very complex question. I've tried not to dodge the tough questions in the past, so let me try to address this one.

A quick thought before I begin. First, Christians don't deny that a meaningful answer to the problem must be found, but do those who deny God have a better answer to the problem of evil and suffering? When asked the question their silence is often deafening.

The Bible, on the other hand, gives a good deal of attention to the reality of suffering. It's not hidden or dismissed. In the Old Testament there are many questions about suffering. The books of Jeremiah, Habakkuk and Job have a lot to say on the subject. Almost one third of the Psalms, the prayers of the Old Testament, are cries that come from discouragement, pain or doubt.

When we come to the New Testament, however, we don't seem to find the same questions we find in the Old Testament. Not that they are completely eliminated, but there's a peace, confidence, hope and joy, not seen in the Old Testament, that even the greatest suffering cannot overwhelm. Something has made a dramatic difference. The answer is clear: in the New Testament, God has a face. He makes himself known in the person of Jesus.

To build a framework for this discussion of evil and suffering, let me talk about love and freedom. Christians believe that we were created to exist in a loving relationship with God and with others. However, love cannot exist if there is no freedom to choose. If you want someone to love you, you can't force them into it. You can't say, "You must love me!" We may sometimes wish it worked that way, but it doesn't. In creating us, God loved us enough to give us the freedom to reject that love.

The problem is we've taken that freedom and distorted it. We've turned away from God and misused this gift of free will. Instead, we've chosen alternatives to God. Isaiah 53:6 tells us, "We all, like sheep, have gone astray; each of us has turned to his own way."

We are not only free to walk away from God, we are free to stay away. Many of the things that you struggle with when it comes to Christianity are brought about by people's own choices. Suffering was not God's choice; it was ours.

The freedom to choose leads us to another problem—the problem of evil. The question you raised is actually twofold, the problem of suffering and the problem of evil. Take a moment to reflect: who is responsible for most of the suffering in the world? Who was responsible for the suffering in World War I, World War II, for the genocide in Rwanda and Darfur? Who is responsible for the

> **genocide:** deliberate and systematic extermination of a national, racial or cultural group

ecological destruction of our planet—the pollution of our oceans and the stripping of our forests? Who is responsible for the pain of your past and your current suffering? I would submit to you that not all suffering is caused by human action, but the large majority of it is.

I love when people say to me, "Well, if there's a God, then why are children starving in Africa?" I once did a research paper on starvation in the world and how it comes about. I learned something startling: The U.S. and Canada could feed the entire world twice over every day. Why don't we? The reasons come down to economics and politics, both in our country and in the poorer nations. It is OUR CHOICE! Now when people ask me how children can be starving in Africa if there is a God, my response is, "Watch your tone of voice, because that is going to be the first question God asks you when you get to heaven." People are starving all over the world because human beings have made the choice to allow them to starve.

The Bible teaches that we are free, responsible beings and with that freedom we choose evil over good, selfishness over love, willfulness over God. We make those choices and then we blame God for the consequences.

The Bible emphasizes strongly the link between suffering and evil. We live in a fallen world and we are a fallen and corrupted race. We are capable of so much good, but somehow, given time, we seem to spoil what we touch. We may often feel morally superior to others, but the reality is every one of us is part of the problem. We like to think that it's everyone else; it's "those people" who cause suffering— but we need not look beyond our own hands and hearts to see the cause of suffering in this world.

People ask, "Well, why doesn't God just wipe out suffering and evil? He's all powerful, isn't he?" The answer is simple: to end suffering, God would have to eliminate the cause of most suffering—you and me. That's why God has not yet intervened to put an end to evil and suffering once and for all. The Bible makes it clear that one day he will, but that time has not yet come. In his grace, mercy and patience God gives us the opportunity to change our hearts. He is a patient God, and he desires to have a relationship with each one of us. He waits for us to turn to him.

It is because of this inseparable link between suffering and evil that God could not deal with one without taking care of the other. God's plan is not to wipe out those who cause the suffering; God's plan is to show mercy and grace to those who cause suffering and call them to come to him and turn from their ways.

Just a quick side note. I know that not all suffering is caused by man. We live in a fallen creation. It's not only man that has fallen, but also the entire natural world. That corruption leaves us in a world filled with defects, catastrophes, disease, and deterioration. We can discuss the implications of this at a later time; I just wanted to mention it.

If you don't believe in God it may be hard to understand, but for me I can have peace knowing that God is just and has already acted to deal with the problem of evil, regardless of its origin, through Jesus Christ. In doing so he has ultimately guaranteed the removal of suffering. Richard Halverson, former chaplain to the U. S. Senate, said, "He was the Great Physician, and in the finest tradition of medical science, he was unwilling to remain preoccupied with the symptoms when he could destroy the disease. Jesus Christ was unwilling to settle for anything less than elimination of the cause of all evil in history."

God chose to enter human history in the person of Jesus Christ, and Jesus certainly knew suffering. He was born in a stable with the animals, and spent his early years in a country not his own. He grew up without recognition or privilege, and worked as a carpenter, or, more likely, a stone mason. He was poor and as an adult in his public ministry never had the comforts we enjoy.

Throughout his ministry he was accused of being a deceiver, a law breaker, a glutton, a heretic, a drunkard and demon possessed. He was attacked and ridiculed for caring about prostitutes, tax collectors and sinners. He was kicked out of the synagogue and it seemed every time he turned around someone threatened to stone him or even

> **heretic:** a person who has beliefs contrary to those taught by his or her church

throw him over a cliff. Finally he was betrayed, deserted by those closest to him, endured a brutal flogging, and was nailed publicly to a wooden cross.

Isaiah tells us, "He was despised and rejected by mankind, a man of suffering, and familiar with pain" (Is. 53:3). My point is this: if Jesus is God, as the Bible teaches, then God understands suffering. Yet the physical and mental suffering I have described pales into insignificance beside another kind of suffering that Jesus endured on the cross. "Christ carried the burden of our sins," we read in 1 John 2:2. In some remarkable way, when Jesus hung on the cross he was taking on his own shoulders the consequences of the evil of the human race.

If you can step back and try to see this from an eternal perspective, the answer begins to take shape. *The God who gave us the freedom to choose has now taken upon himself the consequences of our wrong choices.* Peter writes, "For Christ died for our sins once and for all, the righteous for the unrighteous, to bring you and me to God." Jesus suffered at the point of our greatest need. And that, for him, meant the greatest possible suffering.

The problem of reconciling human suffering with a loving God is only without solution if we don't truly understand the meaning of love. For the Christian, a true understanding of love begins at Jesus' death on the cross.

In his book *Why Do People Suffer?* James Jones tells the story of a school that collapsed, killing all the teachers and most of the children. One little boy was badly injured and rushed to the hospital. For hours a team of doctors and nurses did everything they could to save his life while his mother waited anxiously outside the operating room. After seven hours of surgery, the little boy died.

Instead of letting someone else go out to tell the mother of her loss, the surgeon went himself. As he broke the horrible news the mother became hysterical in her grief and pain and attacked the surgeon. She beat on his chest with her fists. But he didn't push her away. Instead, the doctor held her to himself tightly until her uncontrollable sobbing ended and she rested exhausted in his arms.

In that moment the surgeon began to weep with this mother. Tears streamed down his face as his own grief overwhelmed him. What no one knew was that he had come to the hospital right after learning that his only son had been killed in the same tragedy at the school.

I know people may feel angry with God at times, but he has not dismissed himself from suffering. He's not some cosmic spirit floating around watching it all from a distance, but he understands and even enters into suffering with us. John 3:16 reminds us, "For God so loved the world that he gave his one and only Son, that whoever believes in him shall not perish but have eternal life."

Archbishop of Canterbury William Temple once put it like this: "'There cannot be a God of love,' people say, 'because if there was, and he looked upon the world, his heart would break.' The church points to the Cross and says, 'It did break.'"

The Christian understanding and attitude toward suffering is seen in the context of the cross. Evil and suffering are ultimately conquered through the death and resurrection of Jesus. His resurrection is the exclamation point: It is finished! It is done! One day suffering will no longer exist!

What I am trying to point out is that the answer to the problem of suffering is not a concept; it's a person. When we raise the question of suffering we raise it in the context of some*one*—why did *God* – why doesn't *God*—? Not some*thing*, not some idea, not some philosophical concept, but a person—God. We don't just ask the question in a vacuum, but within a relationship. God's answer was not just to give us words, but to give us a person—Jesus.

When we suffer we need relationship, not philosophy. Emily, I truly believe this is at the heart of the question. The Bible tells us to weep with those who weep, to enter into the suffering of others. All of the intellectual answers I can give you pale in comparison to the reality of divine or even human compassion and comfort.

Even if I could give you a reason for *why* you lost your child, for example, and show you all the good that came from the loss, it wouldn't eliminate your suffering. The mind can never totally reconcile what the heart can experience.

You see evil and suffering as a stumbling block for believers, and I agree that it causes people to pause and think. But in the end, I believe the biblical answers are logical, rational and coherent. The alternative again leaves the questioner empty as he ponders the reality of nothing.

I'm sure I haven't answered all of your questions adequately, but as we have said before, we have time. Your response will allow me to see the gaps that need to be filled and I look forward to the opportunity.

 **Emily**
June 7

I find all the discussion of reasons for evil/suffering in the face of god simply flat. Unconvincing. And here are my thoughts on your last post:

You say: "In creating us, God loved us enough to give us the freedom to reject that love." So God is punishing us for not choosing him? Or, I should say, God is ALLOWING us to suffer for not choosing him? Doesn't sound like a loving god to me. At least not the loving God of the New Testament. More like the vengeful God of the Old Testament, whom people have to beg—er, pray to—for mercy.

 **Jeff Greer**
June 8

If there is a God, and if he gave us free will, and if we chose to reject him and if free choice comes with consequences, how would you suggest he respond? Choice comes with consequences. That's the nature of life.

Also, once we chose to reject him, his response was not to kill us all but to provide a second chance through Christ. Humanity makes a choice, Jesus takes the consequences of that choice on the cross; we get eternal life—how cruel. (Sorry, I couldn't help it.) I know you don't agree with the implications, but God's plan and my thoughts are not illogical.

The God of the New Testament is the same God as the God of the Old. You may not like or agree with the Bible, but Jesus does not contradict what is taught in the Old Testament. You see God from one perspective and it taints your entire thought process, and one day I'm going to figure out why.

You spend most of your time reading people who do not believe in God, and their slant on the Bible. I've been reading some of the same people. They see a possible contradiction in scripture and come to a conclusion based on their existing presupposition—no God—and, aha! more ammo. I see the same possible contradiction and search for an answer, and usually find one. I admit that I'm searching for truth based on my belief that God is real. I also admit that I sometimes come to a place where I need to believe by faith; we all do. But my faith is not a blind leap. If there is a question, I try to find the answer. I guess what I'm saying is that if you don't believe in God then all faith sounds illogical. Your base of understanding is "religion"—what you observe from the outside or by reading the opinion of others. My understanding comes from a study of God's character. Based on his character I see the purpose and plan of God working throughout the Old and New Testament.

I keep using the term "eternal perspective," and I know you don't completely understand it, but it's the lens you must see a Christian worldview through or you'll miss it. This world is not my home. It is not my final destination. My physical life is a vapor, a mist that is here one day and gone the next. I am here to serve God and others with my whole heart, to fulfill my purpose, to live my life with relentless passion and then spend eternity with him.

Many of your concerns and questions about cruelty in the Bible are based upon your view of not only God, but life; it's your view of what's fair, right, just and good based on a temporal perspective, your concept of morality projected on God.

If there is no God, then you don't need to get upset or worked up about evil and suffering; like you say, it's just luck. But if there is a

God, can't you step back and realize that his plan is better than yours or mine, that he loves people more than you ever could? Is it possible that where your finite mind ends his is just beginning? If God is real and he says, "In all things God works for the good of those who love him, who have been called according to his purpose," why can't you trust that it's true? In the end he will work it all out according to his perfect character.

I'll admit that I don't have all the answers, and when I get to heaven my "theology" will be straightened out, but I am sure that God is not cruel, heartless, evil or sadistic. Think about it: Jesus is God, and he was none of those things.

Emily

June 10

You ask who is responsible for most of the suffering in the world. And then you cite wars, deforestation, hunger.

People cause suffering through war. Yes, indeed they do. But few and far between are the political leaders that make those horrible decisions to go to war. Christians, Muslims, Jews and atheists ALL take up arms and fight in the name of their country/faith/values. These soldiers are not turning away from god when they fight. They usually believe they are doing GOD'S WILL!

What's more is this—and this is really important: most suffering is NOT caused by humans, it is caused by mother nature. Here are some examples:

- 300,000,000 (yes, 300 MILLION) have died worldwide from smallpox in the 20th century alone.
- 100,000,000 killed by the Plague during Renaissance.
- 200,000,000 killed by measles in the last 150 years worldwide. 100,000,000 killed by Spanish flu in ONE year 1918-1919—approximately 500,000 in America.
- In the last 30 years, AIDS has killed approximately 30 million people.

- Malaria kills approximately 1,000,000 people per year, mostly children.

Disease getting you down? Let's take a look at some weather-related suffering:

- 230,000+ deaths from tsunami in Indian Ocean, 2004.
- 1,000,000-4,000,000 dead from 1931 flood in China
- Another Chinese flood in 1887 leaves nearly 2,000,000 dead.

Throw in heat waves, earthquakes, tornados, hurricanes, droughts and blizzards, and the Holocaust looks like a cake walk.

 **Jeff Greer**
June 12

A Pharisee once tested Jesus with this question: "Teacher, which is the greatest commandment in the Law?" Jesus replied, "'Love the Lord your God with all your heart and with all your soul and with all your mind.' This is the first and greatest commandment. And the second is like it: 'Love your neighbor as yourself.' All the Law and the Prophets hang on these two commandments." (Matthew 22:34-40)

Jesus' words are not a suggestion; they are how we SHOULD live. What does this have to do with disease? The answer is simple: If we put human life first, loving our neighbor as ourselves, we could save millions of lives. Here are a few examples:

- Edward Jenner discovered that inoculation with cowpox gave immunity to smallpox in 1796. That's 1796, not 1996 or 2006. It was an immense medical breakthrough and has saved countless lives. If we cared, if we loved other children the way we love our own, millions more would have been saved.
- Measles vaccine became available in 1963, and an improved vaccine in 1968. The combination measles-mumps-rubella (MMR) vaccine became available in 1971. How many in the U.S. died from measles after 1971? I would be curious. And how many died around the world, because they had no

- access to the vaccine? Our answer: "We can't just give it away."
- Measures to prevent malaria have been known since the 1640s. Again, why are any children dying today from this disease? You know they are; I know they are; the rest of the world knows they are; the pharmaceutical companies know they are—and they STILL ARE!

In the United States, the vast majority of people enjoy clean drinking water, proper nutrition, inoculations, and good medical care—all important in preventing disease. Why don't we offer that to the rest of the world? Because PEOPLE PREVENT IT! Our system prevents it.

It is not impossible to eliminate most of the deaths you list. In the village we work with in Nigeria, the people are not dying of malaria, AIDS or other common diseases and medical issues. Why? Because we drill wells, we give inoculations, we give medication for AIDS, and they have nutritious food, education, and preventive medical care. That's just one church saving thousands of lives.

Since 2000, more than one billion children in high-risk countries were given the MMR vaccine in mass vaccination campaigns. As a result, global measles deaths have decreased drastically. But why did this take us 30 years?

People are dying every day and most people would not lift a finger—literally—to help. We sit in our big houses with all of our stuff and DO NOTHING. Those with political power do little or nothing. But when people decide to act, they are capable of reducing much suffering in the world.

You said, "But few and far between are the political leaders that make those horrible decisions to go to war." What's worse—to go to war, or to passively sit back and watch millions upon millions of people die over the centuries? The SIN of omission is as bad as the SIN of commission! It's all wrong, and it's all choice.

> People are still dying of measles—why?
>
> People are still dying of malaria—why?
>
> People are still dying of diarrhea—why?

> People are still dying of AIDS—why?
>
> Children are starving to death—why?

You are stinking right children are dying—WHY? Because most people just don't care enough to change it.

As for weather-related suffering, just a few quick thoughts:

- Do we have the technology to warn people about tsunamis?
- Could we create better housing for people so when an earthquake hits, their houses don't crumble like sand?
- Could the Chinese government stop people from living in shacks in death zones right on the river, knowing the floods are coming?
- Did the U.S. have the technology and money to build a stronger wall in New Orleans?

Please don't think I'm saying that humans could have prevented everything, but let's at least be fair and balanced.

It's always after a disaster that people start asking the question, "Could this have been prevented?" Often the answer is yes, but in the end we face the cold hard reality of humanity: it would have cost a lot of money.

The question you're asking is, "Why does God allow earthquakes, tornados, hurricanes, tsunamis, and other natural disasters?" If you don't believe in God or the Bible it's hard to explain a fallen world, but I'll try, if for no other reason than to at least give you my worldview.

I do find it interesting that natural disasters are often termed "acts of God" while no credit is given to God when we have peaceful weather, which is most of the time. God created the whole universe and the laws of nature (Gen. 1:1). Most natural disasters are a result of these laws at work. Tornados, hurricanes and typhoons are the results of weather patterns colliding. Earthquakes are the result of the shifting of the earth's plates. A tsunami is caused by an underwater earthquake.

The Bible teaches that Jesus Christ holds all of nature together (Col. 1:16-17). Could God prevent natural disasters? Yes! Does God sometimes influence the weather? Yes, we see this in James 5:17 and Deuteronomy 11:17. Numbers 16:30-34 shows us that God sometimes causes natural disasters as a judgment against sin.

Is every natural disaster a punishment from God? No.

In much the same way that God does not stop every person from committing evil acts, God allows the earth to reflect the consequences sin has had on creation. Romans 8:18-21 tells us, "I consider that our present sufferings are not worth comparing with the glory that will be revealed in us. The creation waits in eager expectation for the sons of God to be revealed. For the creation was subjected to frustration, not by its own choice, but by the will of the one who subjected it, in hope that the creation itself will be liberated from its bondage to decay and brought into the glorious freedom of the children of God."

The fall of humanity into sin affected everything, including the world in which we live. Everything in creation is subject to "frustration" and "decay." Sin is the ultimate cause of natural disasters, just as it is the cause of disease, death, and suffering.

But the Bible is clear that one day God will bring an end to all evil and suffering. That is a simple explanation and I would be willing to dive in deeper if you would like.

Emily
June 14

Should we talk about kids with cancer, deformities, and the victims of accidents?

Jeff Greer
June 14

We can, and I have answers—do you?

Emily
June 14

Did the dead, maimed and orphaned CHOOSE to walk away from God? I don't think so.

Jeff Greer
June 15

Some do, but from an eternal perspective, if maimed or orphaned people have a relationship with God they will spend eternity with him. Suffering is temporary; relationship is eternal. When you think with only a temporal mind you miss the larger picture. If I'm right, our temporary suffering will mean nothing when compared to our time with God.

Emily
June 16

You make a small "mention" that yes, there are other kinds of pain and suffering, but it seems to pale in comparison to the evil caused by man.

Does it?

Are those who die/suffer from natural disaster or disease just pawns so that we can all learn a lesson and come to know Jesus?

Jeff Greer
June 17

I don't believe that, and that is not what the Bible teaches. That is your false view of God. Your presupposition is that God is evil; my presupposition is that God is good. You see everything through glasses with negative spiritual lenses. If you could see God as good and loving, and try to answer your own questions from that perspective, you might see things differently.

Emily, I have in no way exhausted the answers to your questions. This is just Jeff Greer, the long-haired kid from New City, trying his best to answer some profound questions. There are those, including yourself, that could answer them even better if you took the time to investigate. If you chose to dig until you found a satisfying answer I believe you would change your own mind. For now I will do my humble best to keep writing—sincerely hoping that the Spirit is moving my hand.

You ask if those who die/suffer from natural disaster or disease are just "pawns" so that we can all come to know Jesus. You may not understand suffering, and I may not be able to explain it completely, but Jesus can and one day will, and I'm sure that our torment will not be his answer. God is not torturing people to force them to accept him. Jesus spent much of his earthly ministry healing the sick and suffering. Your question makes no logical sense. When Jesus was here he showed the character of God. Your position would be completely out of character.

Emily

June 18

This is what I want to know: Can you look into the eyes of a parent of a child who is diagnosed with cancer and really, honestly say that God wants their child to suffer and die because he has a greater plan? or he's testing their faith? or punishing someone? It's cruel.

Jeff Greer

June 20

God does not "WANT" their child to suffer and die. If you don't believe my theological views, at least be fair with my explanation. It was not his choice that children suffer and die; that was a result of the choice mankind made in Genesis when they rejected God's instruction. Because we live in a fallen world all of us are suffering the consequences, including our children. Don't blame God for our choices and their consequences. But according to my worldview God can turn any hardship into something that will benefit and strengthen me. Romans 8:28 tells us, "And we know that in all things God works for the good of those who love him, who have been called according to his purpose." His desire, once again, is to offer his plan of life and relationship.

And yes, I can and have had to look parents in the eyes and tell them that God loves them and their child. I have to tell them that I don't understand why this is happening to their child, but I do know that God feels their pain and that he will never leave them or forsake them. That he will comfort them during this terrible time. That I will pray for them and walk with them through it. And that, yes, God has a plan, though we may not see it now; that our God can take the worst of circumstances and make something beautiful from it. I tell them what Jesus said in Matthew 11:28-30, "Come to me, all you who are weary and burdened and I will give you rest. Take my yoke upon you and learn from me, for I am gentle and humble in heart, and you will find rest for your soul. For my yoke is easy and my burden is light." *God* never said that he wants a child to suffer and die because he has a greater plan; that is not a biblical position. He sent his own son to suffer and die instead. I tell parents that God will give them a peace that passes all understanding. And then I cry with them.

I can't know if God is punishing someone, so I would never say that to anyone.

God does test our faith sometimes, yes—but I have never found it to be cruel. This is another long discussion, one worth having. I can't always discern if God is testing someone's faith, so I would never tell someone that is why their child is sick.

God does punish evil and sin. I don't find that to be cruel, either; I think to *not* punish evil is cruel.

What's cruel is a life with no purpose, meaning or value, where the answer to every difficult question is "luck." Emily, you have to ask yourself—what would you say to those same parents?

Emily

June 21

I would rather remain silent than to invent some cruel fantasy that just raises more questions. For me, it's much more logical and satisfying to accept that it's just good, old-fashioned LUCK (or lack of luck) that "explains" why one person gets sucked up in a tornado while the neighbor does not; one child contracts malaria while his brother is spared; one house is bombed while the other stands; one soldier takes a bullet and only loses a leg, while the other loses his life. It makes me feel GRATEFUL to have what I have.

I'm not grateful TO, I am grateful FOR.

Life happens. We are the ones who apply the meaning, lessons, grief, worry, gratitude, and laughter.

And sometimes we even invent religions.

Jeff Greer

June 21

Do you actually believe that telling someone it was luck is more compassionate than what I would share? I can tell you it's *not* more "satisfying." I don't believe what I share is a fantasy, and neither do they. When someone's child is sick, I try not to give pat answers, just comfort. But I do try to answer the questions they ask.

Emily, when you sit with people who are going through a tragedy, I promise you, "Life happens" is not what they want to hear or need to hear. When life brings suffering, God is the one who brings meaning, lessons, purpose, beauty, promise, hope, joy, contentment and peace. I think Paul put it best in Philippians 4:11-13: "I am not saying this because I am in need, for I have learned to be content whatever the circumstances. I know what it is to be in need, and I know what it is to have plenty. I have learned the secret of being content in any and every situation, whether well fed or hungry, whether living in plenty or in want. I can do everything through him who gives me strength."

I was reading *There is a God*, a great book by Antony Flew. He rejected God at the age of 15 because of the question of suffering, but he also remembered what he learned from C.S. Lewis's Socratic Club at Oxford: "Always follow the evidence wherever it leads." His journey brought him back to God after living as an atheist. Why? Because he followed the evidence. The man is no irrational fool, and he had every reason to hold on to his worldview—every reason but one: an honest, intellectual and heartfelt search would not allow him to.

You say it's irrational and illogical to believe, and for reasons you've shared you have chosen to reject faith in God. You're comfortable having no answers to some of life's most profound questions (Who am I? Why am I here?), but those who try to search for answers wherever the evidence may lead are not irrational or illogical; we are just searching for truth.

I would rather spend the rest of my life searching for the truth than rest my mind on the thought that "Luck" is my final answer.

Thank you for pushing me to search even deeper.

More from Jeff

When people ask you how could there be suffering and evil if there's a loving God, most are not looking for some deep intellectual answer. They want to know the whys, but that won't eliminate their suffering. People ask questions because they want answers for the longings in their hearts, not just their minds. They're looking for an understanding that goes beyond the mind. They're looking for true intimacy, for relationship.

When people ask you these questions, you shouldn't be intimidated. Most people aren't looking for a philosophical debate with you; they're looking for a legitimate, honest answer. If we have answers, we need to give them—in a way that touches the heart.

For further study on this topic, read Ravi Zacharias's book *Cries of the Heart.*

4/ who determines right & wrong?

AS a pastor I sometimes find myself surrounded by people who think the same way I do or read books filled with "straw men" that are easy to set up and knock down, but after these last posts with Emily I quickly realized I wasn't in Kansas anymore. These conversations were different. They were real, and at times I felt inadequate to answer such profound questions. I asked God to give me wisdom and discernment, because I knew Emily's questions were not going to get any easier. I wasn't worried about winning an argument; I was more concerned about trying to give answers that would have a meaningful impact. I wasn't fighting with an adversary; I was sharing with a friend, a friend who had helped change the course of my life. Her questions were honest and from the heart, and I prayed my answers would be as well.

I also had to admit to myself that Emily made some very good points. I may not agree with them, but they address some of the same questions I had wrestled through early in my own faith journey. I've come to the realization that it's okay to ask questions, to debate, to struggle, to reason, to try and understand truth, because without the endeavor we will never grow. I also recognize a weakness in how Christians often express our faith. When we are talking with nonbelievers, or even believers, we need to be careful not to throw around "God talk" without understanding our audience or thinking through the implications of our words. For example, we need to be careful and considerate when we talk about and thank God for how he saved one person from a disaster while another died during the same event. Our words can come off flippant or thoughtless. We need to praise God for his mercy, while being prepared to answer the tough "why" questions with compassion. "Why did God take my friend or relative (or let them die) and spare yours?" Emily expressed the same frustration with the standard Christian responses that I've heard from many others. These are difficult questions that deserve a thoughtful answer. I think we can all agree with that.

Emily

June 24

Regarding right and wrong, ethics. That's easy. It's 100% culturally determined. And I suppose it's subjective to some extent, but it's not necessarily individually subjective. It can easily be collectively subjective. It's a communal agreement of acceptable behavior based on survival and custom. Not to be too graphic, but take the example of some forms of female mutilation practiced widely in parts of Africa. What nearly every other culture on earth would consider to be mutilation, evil, humiliation, child abuse, etc., is revered and celebrated as a rite of passage.

Jeff Greer

June 25

When it comes to determining right and wrong, I don't think I could disagree more—no surprise. First, only if there is a God can anything be 100%. That would constitute an absolute. Without God there are no absolutes; everything is relative. If there is a God, then it is he who determines right and wrong, not any individual or culture.

Different cultures may have their own rules that govern behavior, but those will change with time and they depend on who is in power. Every culture has a base of power, and it is usually the strong imposing their will on the weak. In the case of the women being mutilated, I can assure you that if those women had a choice, with no concern for retaliation, they would not be lining up.

As I have traveled I've seen it over and over. One group imposes

> **relative:** existing or having its specific nature only by relation to something else; not absolute or independent

their will on another and calls it "right." In more modern terms, "might makes right." In India, for example, the caste system seems completely right to those in positions of power.

The ruling group creates traditions and customs that allow those in power to remain there. If someone gets out of line, he or she is rejected by the culture and becomes an outcast (or worse). Now the dissenter faces a choice: do I go along without question, or do I stand up for what I believe is right and risk my life?

We see examples throughout history of people standing up for what's right and changing cultural norms. Many have had the courage to risk reprisal or death to bring about change, like Rosa Parks refusing to sit in the back of the bus.

I know from experience that when you get a person alone you hear the cries of their heart. People are generally the same and, given a choice, they would rather not be mutilated (or enslaved, or forced into whatever the culture is pushing). That is why God speaks so strongly about the strong oppressing the weak. The Bible is filled with references to how we should treat those in weaker positions.

It's easy for intellectuals sitting in classrooms (not you) to come up with theories based upon what they see from the outside and take it at face value. I find it interesting that when a country is liberated the truth comes out. *If you want to know the truth of cultural ethics, talk to those who have no power to effect change.* There have been cultures throughout history that believed human sacrifice was right. I wonder how the person being sacrificed felt.

If you don't believe in God you must explain morality, right and wrong, good and bad in human terms. I find this theory convenient but weak when you study each culture over a period of time.

Each person has the law of God written on their hearts and there are universal truths that every culture holds to—that murder for enjoyment is wrong, for example. In the end Hitler was wrong regardless of how many Germans went along with him.

> **caste system:** the rigid Hindu system of social classification passed from one generation to the next

Emily
June 27

You make a series of assumptions which I don't accept: 1) that there is such a thing as absolute good/evil; 2) that there is such a thing as a Moral Law; 3) that for there to be moral law, there must be a moral law maker, aka God.

1) Disagree. 2) Really disagree. 3) Really, really disagree.

The conclusions that follow from these assumptions are rendered false. Although I do appreciate the PROCESS of the argument itself as a sort of Platonic exercise.

Your argument falls apart on the same basis that you argue against mine: It ALWAYS has to do with semantics and bias. Your "absolute right/wrong" is based on YOUR interpretation of God's will, or YOUR understanding of the Bible.

Morality is a physiological, social and particularly human phenomenon. It has more to do with language, survival, and our ability to understand our relationship to each other and to time than any intrinsic quality. No belief in God is required for moral understanding or behavior. To say otherwise is plainly false and borders on offensive to the non-believer. Ironically, the reliance on the faulty notion has often resulted in quite the contrary amoral behavior noted previously.

Some say that our morality makes us unique among animals. Perhaps. The fact that we are keenly aware of the past-present-future continuum, hence our own mortality, is indeed unique. One byproduct of this awareness is the god concept. (I know you disagree). Religion is simply the social/culture structure that has been developed to support the belief.

You make it sound like we "make up a morality" like it's a game. No, it's a social contract, a matter of physiological survival, reciprocation,

> **Platonic:** Relating to the philosophy of Plato, an ancient Greek who questioned the reality of the material world

kinship, satisfaction, predictability. It's instinctual. We don't NEED to invent a God to explain it, although apparently we have, again and again. A recent *Time* magazine article survey showed that populations with high levels of "organic atheism" (that is, not coerced) have some of the highest levels of societal health: low homicide rates, low poverty rates, low infant mortality rates, and low illiteracy rates, as well as high levels of educational attainment, per capita income, and gender equality.

Avoiding another's pain and suffering is NOT the reason for disbelief (although it might make you feel better to think so). It's so much simpler than that. It just doesn't make sense. It's not emotionally, intellectually, spiritually, morally satisfying in any way. That's all she wrote.

Jeff Greer

June 28

The moral dilemma comes in when non-believers pose moral questions to try and disprove the existence of God: "How can a loving God allow evil?"

Help me understand. If there are no absolutes, how do you define right and wrong? If you say that it is determined by the individual or culture (which is relative), then how can you impose that moral code on God or anyone else? When Christians do that they are attacked for being intolerant, dogmatic and judgmental. I just don't understand the double standard. It's hard to keep score when the game keeps changing.

How can you charge God with immoral behavior? If we as humans are allowed to define right and wrong as we see fit, why is God not afforded the same right? And when he does define them, who are we to judge? Why even bring up the question to prove any point? It's illogical.

So you believe humans create morality and then make up God to explain it? You're right; I don't agree. But you're still my friend and I would love to talk about evil. Let's keep beating this around for a little longer. I still don't understand your position completely and I really want to.

I want to make sure that I'm not offending you personally when I question what I see as your position. I know it's a fine line when you discuss these things, but I want to stay on the right side of the line. I know we discussed the offending thing before, but I just wanted to check in.

Emily

June 28

No offense taken on any front. Likewise I'm sure! Helping my daughter make brownies, but I do want to respond to your last comment about your confusion. Since I stopped believing, I have clarity, and since you started believing, you have clarity! Isn't that funny?

I'm not sure why you think there is any moral dilemma whatever for nonbelievers. Nothing leaves us with nothing but ourselves. That's good enough for me.

My morality tells me that war is wrong. Murder is wrong. Terrorism is wrong. Intimidation is wrong. I don't need God or the Bible to tell me that these things are wrong, when I've got a brain, eyes and a heart to show me.

Your postulation that it is a moral universe is unfounded. That is, there is no more morality in a bit of black matter 10,000 light years from here than in a bucket of spit on a porch in West Virginia. Morality is a HUMAN assessment of value. I don't think nonbelievers pose the origin question in terms of morality. Rather, the contrary: The conjecture by believers is a bit maddening, not to mention unnecessarily elaborate.

 **Jeff Greer**
June 30

If you are correct that there is no more morality in a bit of black matter 10,000 light years from here than in a bucket of spit on a porch in West Virginia, I would strongly disagree with your position and understanding of morality. In your view morality has no foundation other than what man decides, collectively or individually. You say, "If we can determine a collective understanding of goodness, for example" and "it's a social contract, a matter of physiological survival: reciprocation, kinship, satisfaction, predictability. It's instinctual." Your concept of morality is like shifting sand; as long as we all agree, it's moral. Without absolutes you are being carried along by cultural norms, your feelings and time. You may find that comforting; I do not.

I would argue that as soon as an atheist makes a moral judgment on the right or wrong of something they are being hypocritical. Where does the "we" get the collective understanding of "goodness?" Atheists say the foundation is instinctual. Why do they say that? Because we are moral beings created in the image of God, and even if we reject him we cannot escape the reality of who we are.

Nietzsche said,

> When one gives up the Christian faith, one pulls the right to Christian morality out from under one's feet. This morality is by no means self-evident. Christianity is a system, a whole view of things thought out together. By breaking one main concept out of it, the faith in God, one breaks the whole. It stands or falls with faith in God.

Though I disagree with Nietzsche in general I have to applaud his honesty. When he "killed God" he was willing to live and die with the consequences. For him it was ultimately insanity.

Just so you know, I talked with my "superhuman sky fairy" (as you call him—LOL) this morning about you and we both love you.

Emily

July 2

In an earlier conversation you made the point that people will often say, "Your truth is your truth because you believe it." Personally I would agree with that.

Jeff Greer

July 2

Emily, My truth is my truth because Jesus said it, because God has written his moral laws on my heart. It doesn't matter what time period I live in, what culture says or what I "feel."

Emily

July 3

But take that one step further: Does your truth deny another's understanding of truth? Does your truth lead you to judge others?

Jeff Greer

July 6

First, the law of non-contradiction states that a truth's opposite cannot also be true. The question of truth is not a "feelings" question or a win-win opportunity. You can be very sincere about your position and be sincerely wrong. When searching for "truth" people shouldn't end up in two different places. When "truth" becomes self-determined, it ceases to be truth and become opinion.

Does my truth lead me to judge others? No, it does not. I may disagree with your view of truth, but that does not cause me to judge you for it. I can make judgments based upon my beliefs without becoming another person's judge.

I can disagree with you and still be tolerant of your views. In fact, to be tolerant, there must be a difference of opinion. I don't understand how people say they're being tolerant when they totally agree with the other person's views. Everyone is tolerant by that definition.

Help me with this line of thinking. You talk as if Christians are the only ones in the world who pass judgment. I'm not saying that Christians never do, but give me a break. Have you read Dawkins, Hitchens, Harris, Nietzsche, Russell—my gosh!

In his book *Letter to a Christian Nation*, Sam Harris writes, "The truth is that many who claim to be transformed by Christ's love are deeply, even murderously, intolerant of criticism. While we may want to ascribe this to human nature, it is clear that such hatred draws considerable support from the Bible." Would you say Harris is "tolerant" of those he is "judging"?

Christopher Hitchens writes of Mother Teresa, "She spent her life opposing the only known cure for poverty, which is the empowerment of women and the emancipation of them from a livestock version of compulsory reproduction." (Christopher H. is judging Mother Teresa—wow! When I googled Christopher Hitchens I found no examples of *him* empowering women, but a lot of examples of women speaking against him.)

The whole "judgmental attitude" argument is frustrating, to say the least. Christians are attacked, ridiculed and belittled all the time in our culture and killed in others. Over 171,000 Christians are martyred each year, and no one ever talks about it. It's open season on believers and no one cares. I'm not looking for sympathy, just an honest discussion of the facts.

> **Christopher Hitchens:** An English author, religious and literary critic, known for criticizing popular religious and political figures

The difference is I can disagree with you and still love you, defend you and lay down my life for you. I have and will continue to defend the rights of others to express their views even when those views are in opposition to my own.

Emily

July 7

Does your truth justify discrimination against homosexuals, Muslims, Hindus, wiccans and non-believers?

Jeff Greer

July 7

No! That is, unless you call disagreement or one's own beliefs "discrimination." Discrimination is defined as "unfair treatment of a person or group on the basis of prejudice," so the answer is without question, NO. I have helped and befriended Muslims, Hindus, homosexuals, witches and warlocks. I don't agree with most of their beliefs or choices, but that does not keep me from loving them. If I stopped loving and helping people I disagreed with I'd be out of a job.

Emily

July 7

My understanding is that a believer's answer to all of these questions is a resounding yes. Meanwhile, I think that most atheists would say no to all of the above. They may throw a "delusional" insult or two along the way, but generally, there is no framework in place for evangelistic activities. Maybe they don't care, or perhaps they concede it's a bit of a lost and unimportant cause.

Jeff Greer

July 8

WOW! How can you make such a claim? Harris and Dawkins (Just to name two) spend most of their waking hours aggressively pushing their worldview.

"A delusional insult or two along the way"? Have you listened to these men? Nietzsche considered the Beatitudes in Matthew 5 to be a damning approach to life. He said they emphasize the responsibility of man toward the poor and weak of society. According to him, a society driven by such an ethic is, in effect, controlled by the losers. So the poor in spirit, those who mourn, the meek, those who are hungry and thirsty, the merciful, the pure in heart, peacemakers and those who are persecuted, are, from his perspective, unworthy examples of what make up a good society?

They think pushing their worldview is "an unimportant cause"? No way—they are passionate about eradicating a worldview based on God. Richard Dawkins wrote, "Only the willfully blind could fail to implicate the divisive force of religion in most, if not all, of the violent enmities in the world today."

You say they have "no framework for those activities"—what? How about print and electronic media, public schools and universities? Most public universities are filled with teachers who ridicule students who believe in God. Dawkins wanted to deny access to Oxford University to anyone who held a creationist worldview.

Come on. They may not use the same terminology, but please don't pretend that atheists don't push their worldview. Please don't tell me that they are just tolerant, open-minded, free-thinking, compassionate "do-gooders" who sit around all day and sing, "All we are saying is give peace a chance."

> **Beatitudes:** The eight sayings of Jesus in the Sermon on the Mount that begin with the word "Blessed."

Emily
July 10

Does your truth tell you that belief in Jesus is the only entry into heaven (John 3:16)?

Jeff Greer
July 10

Yes. Jesus said clearly in John 14:6, "I am the way, the truth, and the life; no one comes to the Father but by me." That is what Jesus said. If I were to say anything to the contrary I would be a hypocrite. It also says, "God desires that none would perish but all come to repentance." It is God's heart that all would spend eternity with him. He came to earth and sacrificed himself because of his love for us. He will give every opportunity for people to respond, and I think we will be surprised who we will see in heaven.

Question: Do you believe that it's right that people will be abused, starved, raped and murdered without finding justice? Do you believe that child molesters and mass murders will go unpunished now (as many do) and never face judgment? Is that "fair," is that moral, right or just? Is it fair that the weak are oppressed by the strong throughout history? Where is the justice? Left to man, injustice will continue unchecked, or enforced only as some people see fit.

I trust God to bring justice and judgment, not man. If you're right—my goodness, what a horror for billions. I guess it's all in how you view the universe.

Emily
July 11

Does your truth tell you that you should pray for others to "see the light" (as if they are in the dark)? Does your truth tell you that some are condemned to hell and suffering? Does it teach you that some are "saved" while others are LEFT BEHIND? Does your truth tell you that Jesus will come again and pass judgment upon mankind?

Jeff Greer

July 11

The answer to these questions is yes. I guess if I'm deciding who to believe— Jesus or Darwin, Harris, Dawkins, Russell, Nietzsche etc.— I'll take Jesus.

Emily

July 13

To what end does that belief take you? Are you willing to scare/confuse children and invoke fear for the sake of believing?

Jeff Greer

July 13

I never do that. We were together in church and that never happened. Our youth pastor never scared/confused us. He never tried to manipulate us.

Emily

July 13

I do think that the concept of hell is a scare tactic—both theologically and politically—sadly used on children and adults, too. Our youth pastor did have us watch a film about the rapture that was very traumatic for me. Very traumatic. Do you remember that? I'm sick over it. I'm quite sure he didn't have a malicious intent, but fear and compliance was the result nevertheless.

Hell is nothing more than a tool of control and cruelty. As the philosopher Seneca said: "To the common man, Religion is Truth; to the sage, Religion is Folly; to the powerful, Religion is Useful."

In fact, reference to God's judgment or wrath upon those non-compliant makes for a rather unattractive deity, wouldn't you agree? Not to mention that anything but universal salvation flies completely in the face of the theoretical omniscient, omnibenevolent and omnipotent God.

Jeff Greer

July 15

I've been thinking about what you wrote concerning our youth pastor. I must have missed that. I agree with you on this one. I remember when Deb and I were youth leaders and took our group on a retreat. They had us review a movie they were going to show that night—the same type of movie you wrote about. We saw it and told them we were not going to show that to our kids (almost all of them were not Christians) because we felt it was not appropriate for our group. They were not happy with our decision, but we didn't care. We had a Bible study with our students while the rest of the camp watched the film.

Deb also saw a movie like that when she was a teen and she reacted the same way you did. We feel that that kind of tactic is emotionally manipulating with few long-term results. I know it's been years, but I'm very sorry for the harm it caused you. It helps me better understand your questions on that subject and the passion behind them.

We never did that in our youth ministry, and we had a group of over 900 students. We met their felt needs and earned the right to be heard. We spoke the truth in love, and now we have people all over the world impacting the lives of others. I don't have a problem defending my faith, but I won't defend behavior I don't agree with.

I like the way you got me to come back to church: smile faces and love. You're quite the evangelist. :)

One last thought. I don't serve God because I fear him; I serve him because I love him for transforming my life.

Emily

July 16

I'm so glad that you and Deb didn't allow your kids to see that film. You ARE a righteous and wise dude! The folks who put that film out, or pressure people like you and Deb to show it, should be ashamed at the very least. It's indefensible, and it makes my heart hurt.

What's worse than child abuse? Well, child abuse in the name of God, of course! A lesson that too many churches haven't seemed to grasp somehow.

I AM the evangelist!! My son calls me an evangelical <u>agnostic</u>. I think I'm just enthusiastic, which as you know, is usually contagious. Achoo! Careful—you might catch something! =)

Jeff Greer

July 16

The word "enthusiastic" has its origin in the Greek word *entheos*, meaning "having God within." I see God in you, and that makes me enthusiastic. (I'm not being sarcastic in that comment—just speaking from the heart.)

I don't think it was the intent of the retreat planners to hurt anyone. They saw the movie as a tool to share a message. I just think it's better to share the message personally, because you have face-to-face interaction and can be more sensitive. The Bible says to speak the truth *in love*. Thoughtful people have the freedom to agree or disagree, but I think the person sharing—whoever it is—needs to try to avoid being offensive.

> **agnostic:** a person who believes that knowledge of God is impossible

More from Jeff

Do you believe that there are some things that are right and some things that are wrong? Why do you believe that? Without God, how can you tell me that I did something wrong? By whose definition? Who decides what's right or wrong? You? Society? Why is your definition of right and wrong any better than Hitler's, Stalin's, Jack the Ripper's, or Osama Bin Laden's?

Who decides? And how do you decide?

In a 1948 debate between Fredrick Copleston and Bertrand Russell, Copleston asked Russell if he believed in good and bad. Russell admitted that he did. Copleston then asked him how he differentiated between the two. Russell said, "The same way that I differentiate between colors."

Copleston said, "But you distinguish colors by seeing, don't you?" How then do you judge between good and bad?" Russell responded, "I do so on the basis of my feelings."

How in the name of reason can you possibly differentiate between good and bad on the basis of feelings? Whose feelings? What if your feelings change? What if my feelings disagree with your feelings?

You see, without God's absolute truth you end up in a philosophical debate or discussion—fun in a class, but not fun in real life. If you claim there's no God, you cannot live out your worldview in the real world. The moment you use the words *right*, *wrong*, *good*, or *bad*, or judge someone in any way, you become a hypocrite.

For me, it's clear. If you say something's right, then you have to assume something's wrong. If you say something's good, then you have to assume something's bad. If you assume right and wrong, good and bad, then you assume a moral law that dictates right and wrong, good and bad. If you assume a moral law, then you assume a moral lawgiver that decides that moral law. That leads us to God, and to absolute truth. Something is good or right not because I feel it, but because God said it.

C.S. Lewis wrote, "The moment we use the word 'better' we assume a point of reference." Without God, there is no point of reference, and words like *good* and *bad*, *right* and *wrong* are meaningless.

As a matter of fact, nonbelievers need to borrow the foundation of a Christian worldview in order to even have a conversation about morality, because without God there is no reference point for the conversation.

In my conversation with Emily I said that atheists naturally use words like *good* and *evil*, *right* and *wrong*, because God has written his law on the hearts of everyone, not just Christians:

> Indeed, when Gentiles, who do not have the law, do by nature things required by the law, they are a law for themselves, even though they do not have the law, since they show that the requirements of the law are written on their hearts, their consciences also bearing witness, and their thoughts now accusing, now even defending them.
>
> - Romans 2:14-15

You can't help but use those terms in the real world because you were created in the image of God, and when you see things that are wrong, your heart cries out. Jeremiah says, "I would speak with you about your justice: Why does the way of the wicked prosper?" (Jer. 12:1) Like Jeremiah, we can't help but get worked up when we see cruelty or abuse; God has put it within us.

It doesn't matter whether you live on an island in the middle of nowhere, or with millions of people in a city; you have God's law written on your heart. There are things we don't need to be taught.

Christians have the added benefit of the Bible in learning how God expects us to treat others. The Christian worldview says I should love my enemy and to do good to those who may harm me:

> But I tell you who hear me: Love your enemies, do good to those who hate you, bless those who curse you, pray for those who mistreat you. If someone strikes you on one cheek, turn to him the other also. If someone takes your cloak, do not stop him from taking your tunic. Give to everyone who asks you, and if anyone takes what belongs to you, do not demand it back. Do to others as you would have them do to you.

> If you love those who love you, what credit is that to you? Even 'sinners' love those who love them. And if you do good to those who are good to you, what credit is that to you? Even 'sinners' do that. And if you lend to those from whom you expect repayment, what credit is that to you? Even 'sinners' lend to 'sinners,' expecting to be repaid in full. But love your enemies, do good to them, and lend to them without expecting to get anything back. Then your reward will be great, and you will be sons of the Most High, because he is kind to the ungrateful and wicked. Be merciful, just as your Father is merciful.
>
> - Luke 6:27-36

Not only are we to treat others with kindness and mercy, but we are to fight for the cause of justice. Psalm 82:2-4 says, "How long will you defend the unjust and show partiality to the wicked? Defend the cause of the weak and fatherless; maintain the rights of the poor and oppressed. Rescue the weak and needy; deliver them from the hand of the wicked."

How do you respond when someone quotes to you "Judge not lest you be judged"? First, let's be clear; most people take this verse out of context. Everyone who breathes and thinks makes judgments every day. I wonder—if I answer someone's question about judgment in a way that is not acceptable to that person, will he judge me for it?

It would seem from listening to nonbelievers that Christians are the most judgmental people on earth, but this is not true. Sam Harris, author of *Letter to a Christian Nation*, believes passionately about working to eliminate religion around the world (not just Christianity). He writes:

> I would be the first to admit that the prospects for eradicating religion in our time do not seem good. Still, the same could have been said about the efforts to abolish slavery at the end of the eighteenth century. Anyone who spoke with confidence about eradicating slavery in the United States in the year 1775 surely appeared to be wasting his time, and wasting it dangerously.

Sam Harris clearly is not taking a nonjudgmental, "live-and-let-live" position. I don't think Harris is saying we should go out and slay all the Christians, but I certainly would say he is passionate about spreading his worldview. This is the same man who said if he had a magic wand and could eliminate either rape or religion, he would eliminate religion.

In my mind I separate Old Atheists from New Atheists. I believe that Old Atheists, like Voltaire, Nietzsche and Russell, were more intellectually honest in their discussion of atheism. Dawkins, Hitchens and Harris are extremely aggressive when presenting their views, while attempting to silence any opposition.

I know I am passionate about what I believe; you should be passionate about what you believe, and those with opposing views can be passionate about what they believe. I have no problem with people being passionate and enthusiastic about what they believe. What's important to understand is that Christians are not the only ones who are sometimes "judging others."

How should we respond when people get red in the face, belittling and belligerent? We should not respond in kind.

Remember Jesus' words: "Love your enemies, do good to those who hate you, bless those who curse you, pray for those who mistreat you. If someone strikes you on one cheek, turn to him the other also. . . . But love your enemies, do good to them, and lend to them without expecting to get anything back."

So how should we answer an agitated skeptic? We should stand up for what we believe, but do it with *gentleness and respect* (I Pet. 3:15). You will never argue someone into the Kingdom of God, especially if your arguments are aggressive and belittling. If you're talking with someone and make them feel awkward and uncomfortable, they immediately put up a wall, and are not open to what you are saying; they simply solidify their position and fire back. Even if people are belligerent and their views are repulsive to you, you must treat them with love, respect, and gentleness, for they are made in the image of God.

People don't come to know Christ just through intellectual debate

> **skeptic:** a person who doubts the truth of Christianity

and discussion. Experiences in their lives with God and other people influence them as well, bringing them to a point in their life where they ask what is really true. The intellect and heart work together. This is true both for those who come to belief and for those who decide to reject God.

No thinking person can avoid the search for answers to life's most challenging questions. Each of us should be a seeker of truth, looking for answers to questions about the whys and hows of life, the meaning and purpose of life, the right and wrong of life. The answer to these significant questions must be based on truth.

5/Atrocities in the name of God

AFTER my discussion with Emily about morality, right, and wrong, I spent a lot of time contemplating her questions and my answers. I think this discussion hit me the hardest. It took me back to my childhood and teen years, before I believed in God.

Even before I was a Christian I struggled with the way people handled truth and morality. I remember being told by many adults that people were "good at heart" and things could often be right or wrong depending on one's perspective. I was told any belief was okay as long as you were sincere.

None of this rang true for me. From my point of view, people who believed everyone was "good at heart" must have lived a sheltered existence. Growing up I found school was filled with people who could be cruel, that adults were often selfish and our elected leaders were almost always dishonest. The idea that right or wrong was based upon an individual's or a culture's perspective left me feeling vulnerable and uneasy. It was like walking in a swamp with bare feet; you can never trust your next step. When I was a child "sincere" adults caused me a lot of pain. Now, as a pastor, I work with many people who've been abused by "sincerity": the "sincere" parent, husband, or wife who promises the next morning to never drink again; the "sincere" father who promises to show up, but leaves you waiting again; the "sincere" single mother, who says she loves you, but then chooses to let predatory men in the house. It wasn't from the Bible that I learned people aren't "good at heart," or that a person's perspective is based on emotions that shift like sand, or that sincerity is not the foundation for truth. I just needed to live and interact with other people to learn those lessons.

But when I gave my life to Christ the world finally made sense. People have a sinful nature, but because they are created in God's image they also have the capacity to do incredibly good things, especially as they become more like Jesus. I learned one's perspective is only valid if it aligns with God's Word, and sincerity is not the litmus test for truth. Emily reminded me that my worldview is validated by reality, not opinion or wishful thinking. My beliefs don't come from what I was taught as a child at church, but from the reality I experience in the world.

Emily

July 20

You wrote: "There have been cultures throughout history that believe human sacrifice was right. I wonder how the person being sacrificed felt."

This is not only history—it is NOW. Every teenage terrorist that straps a bomb to his back and walks into a market or a mosque or onto a school bus is committing human sacrifice in the name of God. To please God. Nineteen young men did it on 9/11 and my friends and neighbors died. From what I understand, they do it with a full and open heart for the promise of reward in heaven. I can only imagine how frustrating that makes you and all God-loving people feel. Holy wars (all faiths) have left a terrible stain on human history and frankly, it's one more reason why I say no thanks, I don't want to join that club.

Jeff Greer

July 21

I totally agree with your frustration with those who kill others in the name of God. There are some religions that encourage that type of behavior. Christ *encourages* belief in him; in other faiths you are *compelled* to believe—believe or die. I see it all the time in Africa. More Christians are <u>martyred</u> today than at any time in history.

> **martyr:** a person who is put to death because of his or her religion

Christians can disagree and live in peace; we have in the U.S. for over 200 years. For others around the world it's submit or die. I would not want to join that club either.

Emily

July 21

But what about the atrocities of the church? The Salem witch hunts, the Crusades. Even my 12-year old can tell you that Europe is littered with the graves of those who died in century upon century at the hand of popes, bishops, queens and kings, all of whom sang the praises of Jesus Christ their savior.

Jeff Greer

July 22

Emily, let me begin by saying that the question is legitimate and deserves a good answer. Church history is filled with terrible atrocities, and not just in early Europe. No one would argue that point. But many atheists claim that this disproves the existence of God, which I find to be an invalid argument.

It is true that there are many examples of evil committed in the name of Christianity. In the past, those who disagreed with church doctrine, such as Galileo, were persecuted or killed. (Side note: official Church doctrine is not the same as biblical truth. The Bible never said the world is flat!) In addition, during the Crusades there were those who committed atrocities that were not sanctioned by God, or the church. In modern times, wars have been fought between Protestants and Catholics in Northern Ireland.

However, if we look below the surface, I would submit that these people were often using religion to justify their own selfish agendas.

Now let me take a few moments to discuss the Crusades. I understand that whatever conclusion we come to will not profoundly change either of our positions, but for me it's a matter of trying to understand the truth. I guess I'm getting more and more tired of people stating opinion as fact, or retelling old narratives disguised as recent discoveries. I think I can sometimes be guilty of the same thing. We often take the lazy man's approach.

It feels like after 9/11 the Crusades have been a topic of conversation. Many have made the assertion that the Islamic world has a just grievance against the U.S. specifically and the West in general.

President Obama at the recent prayer breakfast said,

> Humanity has been grappling with these questions throughout human history. And lest we get on our high horse and think this is unique to some other place, remember that during the Crusades and the Inquisition, people committed terrible deeds in the name of Christ. In our home country, slavery and Jim Crow all too often was justified in the name of Christ.

We hear this same narrative from others who insist that the present violence has its roots in the Crusades' brutal attacks against the cultured and tolerant Muslim world. The crusaders are portrayed as self-righteous, intolerant, imperialist murderers. We are told the entire effort was unjustified and has left a black mark on the history of the Church and Western civilization.

I was flying to Africa a few years ago and talked with a Christian woman on her way home to a Muslim-controlled area of Nigeria. I asked her what it was like for those who go to church in her area. Her answer was sad and sobering. She said, "For the many who live in my state you are either a Muslim or a martyr." I asked her why she continued to openly worship. She said, "When Christ returns I don't want to be found hiding."

Because of my experiences in Africa and what I know the Bible

---

Islamic: Following the Muslim religion, founded by the prophet Muhammad and taught by the Koran; relating to the countries and cultures that follow the Muslim religion

imperialist: exercising the rule or authority of an empire or nation over foreign countries

teaches, I've never been comfortable with the narrative that the Crusades were offensive wars against Islam led by power-mad popes and fought by religious fanatics for land and wealth.

I wanted to know what is historically accurate. What's the truth about the Crusades?

So here's what I've learned: the Crusades to the East were in every way defensive wars in response to Muslim aggression. They were an attempt to fight and retake Christian land from earlier Muslim conquests. Christians in the eleventh century were not a bunch of fanatics bent of conquest; they were being threatened, persecuted and killed under the power of Islam. The first goal of the Crusades was to save their follow Christians, which I believe is a just cause.

Pope Innocent III wrote to the Knights Templar, "You carry out in deeds the words of the Gospel, 'Greater love than this hath no man, that he lay down his life for his friends.'"

The second goal of the Crusades was the liberation of Jerusalem and the other places considered holy. Medieval Crusaders saw themselves as pilgrims. The retaking of Jerusalem was seen as an act of restoration and an open declaration of one's love of God. (Just so you know, I do not believe recapturing land *in and of itself* is a biblical reason to go to war.)

I was always told that the knights took advantage of an opportunity to rob and pillage in faraway lands. But instead of writing of glory, power and money, the knights wrote of self-sacrifice and their love for God. We are told that their words were only a front for their evil plans. We now know that knights were wealthy men with plenty of their own land in Europe. Far from being money-hungry monsters, many of them gave up their wealth to rescue those in need, and some fought because they hoped to store up treasure in heaven. Many had not lived godly lives and saw the Crusades as an opportunity to make amends.

It's easy for people living today to look back and judge those who took up arms to defend their brothers and sisters in Christ. It's hard for us to understand how religious people could fight a war for any reason. Then or now most honest people fight for what they believe to be a good cause, sacrificing for things they hold precious. After all of my study I've come to the conclusion that whether or not we agree with the crusaders, the world we know today would be very different without their decision to stand against the aggression of their time. I don't like war. To see lives taken in any war breaks my heart. But I do believe that war is sometimes necessary to protect lives, and to stand for what is right.

I want to make sure that I'm not just painting a rosy picture. This was war and war is ugly. Not everyone had good intentions and fought for the love of others or God. In 1095, a bunch of Crusaders led by Count Emicho of Leiningen robbed and murdered every Jew they could find. But I also want to point out that the bishops of that area tried to stop them.

I'm sure there were many other godless acts committed by those claiming faith in Christ. I don't need to be a historian or have special insight to come to that conclusion; I just need to understand human nature.

Emily, I'm not looking to debate this topic just for the sake of debate. I guess for me this was something I needed to address because of the inconsistencies in the modern narrative. If I had come to a different conclusion based on the evidence, I can promise you I would have been saddened but satisfied. My faith doesn't rise or fall with the behavior of others.

I hope the family is well. Please give them all my love. Still smiling, Jeff

Emily

July 22

I agree. Butchery of humanity has been done by the millions both in the name of God—Hitler, the Crusades—and in denouncement of God—Stalin, Mao. They're all wrong, and they are all motivated not by theology, but by power.

 **Jeff Greer**
July 23

The answer for their behavior is explained to us in Romans 3:23, "For all have sinned and fall short of the Glory of God." The bottom line is people have a sinful nature.

The problem is we can't overcome our sinful nature on our own. What we need to free ourselves from this dilemma is a savior, and we find that in the person of Jesus Christ.

Once a person gives his or her life to Christ, specific changes take place. Now, do people who believe become sinless? No! Believing makes us more sensitive and aware of our sin, and true followers of Christ repent when they find that they have caused harm to others.

Repent means to be sorry for your sinful behavior, to hate it and to stop it. True believers try, with God's help, to overcome their sinful patterns. This is not to say that Christians are incapable of still causing harm, but when they do they are acting outside of a clear biblical worldview.

You also have the issue of false believers. In John 6:60, after counting the cost of following Jesus, we read, "On hearing it, many of his disciples said, 'This is hard teaching. Who can accept it?'" There are a lot of people who call Jesus Lord, but he sees right through them. You can grow up in church, learn the lingo—and be a great liar.

You talked about the "popes, bishops, queens and kings" who killed others, and all the while "sang the praises of Jesus Christ their savior." I'm sure you're right—some did. And some still do. But does that make them true followers of Christ? Matthew 7:21-23 gives a clear answer:

> Not everyone who says to me, 'Lord, Lord,' will enter the kingdom of heaven, but only he who does the will of my Father who is in heaven. Many will say to me on that day, 'Lord, Lord, did we not prophesy in your name, and in your name drive out demons and

perform many miracles?' Then I will tell them plainly, 'I never knew you. Away from me, you evildoers!'

Jesus knew who was taking his name and using it for evil purposes.

Jesus called his disciples to be humble, loving, kind, compassionate and honest, and he set the example for believers to follow. John says:

> We know that we have come to know him if we obey his commands. The man who says, 'I know him,' but does not do what he commands is a liar, and the truth is not in him. But if anyone obeys his word, God's love is truly made complete in him. This is how we know we are in him: Whoever claims to live in him must walk as Jesus did.
>
> - I John 2:3-6

The bottom line is that not all professing Christians are Jesus' disciples, and that's the problem. When someone chooses to disobey Jesus' clear teaching and causes harm to others, that shame rests squarely on the shoulders of the people who committed the crime, not on Jesus.

There are also those who have created a different church history than the one you describe. These are men and women of character who founded universities, schools and hospitals, people who have served the less fortunate, and who have sacrificed their own lives to help others. These people make up the majority of believers throughout history. When I was in Nigeria early this year I saw the graves of Christians who literally gave their lives in service to God. Not one among them lived past age fifty.

Are there those who have used the name of Christianity to gain power, commit sexual sin, kill the innocent, lie and cause terrible pain? Yes, but I'm sure—because I know what the Bible teaches—not one of those people was walking as Jesus did.

Emily
July 25

In your defense, you point out a clear difference between the "real" Christians who are nonviolent, who follow (some of) Jesus' teachings, and those who claim that they're Christian and fight and kill anyway. I get it. Who wouldn't want to disassociate themselves from bloodlust?

Two things: First, for those who are OUTSIDE of that distinction, a Christian is a Christian is a Christian. That may not be fair, but it's your problem to address. I can imagine how frustrating it must be to have your faith hijacked. But honey, you've got a big, fat, long history to dispel. You may be pushing a rock uphill.

Hitler was more of a Christian than Mao Zedong was a Darwinist, for example. In Mein Kampf, Hitler wrote: "Christ was the greatest early fighter in the battle against the world enemy, the Jews. . . .The work that Christ started but could not finish, I—Adolf Hitler—will conclude."

Jeff Greer
July 26

Emily, do you honestly believe that Jesus' teaching (a Christian worldview) would advocate the killing of anyone in his name? The Hitler quote is perfect—perfectly irrational. Jesus was a Jew and the Bible says that his followers are Jews as well. So I guess we would

---

Mao Zedong: Communist dictator and chairman of the People's Republic of China from 1949-59, responsible for an estimated 40 to 70 million deaths through starvation, forced labor and executions of his own people

Darwinist: one who follows Charles Darwin's theory that new species arise (evolve) from earlier forms through natural selection

Mein Kampf: The autobiography of Adolph Hitler that presented his philosophy and his plan for German conquest

have to kill ourselves—it's illogical madness. Turn the other cheek, love your enemies, think of others as better than yourself—and on and on. Going to war to force our worldview on others is *not* and will *never* be acceptable to Christ.

In the last 100 years those who have followed Darwin's theory to its logical conclusion have killed more people than in any century in the history of the world—fact.

You speak as if Christian history is predominantly filled with bloodthirsty monsters. I would ask that you please step outside of that mindset and consider the rest of the story. Again, those who kill in Jesus' name are in direct opposition to his teaching. Why is it so easy for you to defend Darwin and so difficult for you to see my perspective? Jesus has brought about more good by any definition than anyone who has ever lived. Why is it so easy to point out the misguided and leave out the billions of people who have lived and died serving others throughout history? I feel like I'm debating emotion rather than reason sometimes and I don't completely understand it. You may feel the same. I have learned that the internal heart issues are often much more powerful than the external head issues or objections. Intelligent people on both sides disagree, so that tells me the issues are beyond the intellect.

I'm not perfect, and I'm sure I step outside of my worldview and cause people harm sometimes, but I would hope that when my story is told I will be remembered for more than my mistakes. Beyond that I would hope that people could look beyond my lapse of judgment and seek the truth of Christ's own words.

We've talked a lot about what Christians have "inflicted" on others but we have not talked enough about what their worldview produces. The list of good deeds would take more time than we have. If you just take my life, for example. My desire to defend the weak and alleviate suffering has impacted thousands of lives, and I'm just one person at one point in history. The wells being drilled in Nigeria will save more lives over time than were taken by many of the atrocities described. If there is no God, suffering has no real definition. Like you said, pain and suffering means nothing unless you're a believer.

Religion is not the cause of all the problems in life; people are. Do people misuse religion? Yes—and that makes me angry as well, but it does not disqualify its validity.

Emily

July 27

I would take exception with your statement that those who "follow Darwin's theory have killed people." Darwin was a biologist, not a politician, or a soldier. I think he would have a hard time with SOCIAL Darwinism, if that's what you're referring to. I do too.

Jeff Greer

July 27

I was responding to your insistence that "Christians" cause so much suffering in the world. I'm not blind to the fact that people will use Christ's name to do wrong, but it is in violation of his clear teaching. All people have value. Not just because I feel they do, but because God says they do. His words are clear: "Whatever you did to one of the least of these you did to me." (Matthew 25:40) Killing people is a direct attack on God himself.

Jesus was neither a politician nor a soldier, nor did he ever call upon his followers to defend him. When soldiers came to arrest him and hang him on a cross, he told his disciples not to fight to protect him. They beat him until you could see his insides; they pressed a crown of thorns on his head; they made him carry his own cross; they spit on him, insulted him, taunted him, and then nailed his hands and feet to a cross. And what does he say? "Father, forgive them."

Jesus died for our evil behavior, and he continues to be present every time we inflict suffering upon each other. He is not an outside

> **Social Darwinism:** The belief that Darwin's theory of evolution in nature also applies to society, with the best-adapted individuals or societies prevailing over those that are weaker

observer of our pain, but a participant with us in our pain. Any violation of his teaching is anti-Christ. It doesn't matter if it's Jim Jones, the Pope, Billy Graham, an entire church, or me. Any sinful act that is done by a "Christian" happens outside a biblical worldview, regardless of who the person is.

Emily

July 27

The point I am trying to make is that those who consider THEMSELVES Christian (whether you do or not) have killed plenty, and in the name of God.

Jeff Greer

July 27

Here again is MY point. Darwin's beliefs have established a naturalistic worldview. I'm not saying he advocated killing people. What I'm saying is that when you eliminate God from the equation, man alone determines value. When you leave value—right and wrong—open to opinion or feelings, you end up with specific consequences. Would Darwin like the result? No but it is the outcome of a worldview without God. I may be stuck with "Christians" acting *outside* of a Christian worldview, but consider the problem of people acting the same way *within* a naturalistic worldview.

Given opportunity and time, people will cause suffering. The question is which worldview is true and offers the greatest hope. Where the naturalistic worldview is assumed, it admits to an unknown starting point for life, and therefore for morality as well. You may not like it or agree, but I believe the stone you're pushing is a bit heavier than mine.

More from Jeff

Yes, people who claim to be Christians have committed atrocities in the past. But when we look at statistics from history, we find another side of the story.

University of Hawaii Professor Rudy Rummel spent most of his life studying the causes and conditions of mass violence and war, hoping his work would help stop these atrocities. Prof. Rummel defined democide as the murder of any person or people by a government, including genocide, politicide, and mass murder, but not war-related deaths. Tables 1 and 2 in the Resources section at the back of this book summarize the numbers of people slaughtered by various political groups throughout history.

Before the twentieth century, millions of people were killed by people groups who wanted to eliminate other people groups (remember, these don't include those killed in wars). What percent of these killings were due to religious democide, such as the Crusades and the Spanish Inquisition? It is less than 3% of the totals, dwarfed by millions killed by China and the Mongols and many others. In the Resources section of this book you can read more about the Crusades.

Vox Day, in *The Irrational Atheist*, lists 22 atheistic regimes that committed 153,368,610 murders in the twentieth century alone. During the last hundred years, religious killings were less than 2% of total democides. The top two killers, China and the U.S.S.R., were specifically atheistic regimes (which had never existed before in human history).

Should we blame atheism for more than half of the atrocities committed during the twentieth century? That would probably be unfair. I believe that Darwin's theory just gave those who already had a sinful nature a better excuse for their murderous behavior. Sinful people hungry for power will always find a way to inflict suffering on the innocent and unsuspecting. If one examines the nature of the regimes that committed these atrocities (even the religious ones), the key factor is a lust for power. We see this by the type of governments

> **politicide:** systematic destruction of a people belonging to a specific political movement

committing democide: the vast majority were totalitarian or authoritarian regimes.

When we consider violence due to war, we see a similar pattern. According to Professor Rummel, during the period from 1816 to 2005 there were 205 wars between non-democracies, 166 wars between non-democracies and democracies, and zero wars between democracies. People have a sinful nature. When a few people have absolute control, they live out that sinful nature and the result is often slaughter. Lord Acton's warning that "Power corrupts, and absolute power corrupts absolutely" seems to be right on target. Sinful, power-hungry, money-consumed people are to blame for much of the world's suffering.

Yes, those who claim to follow Christ have caused atrocities. But eradicating religion as some atheists encourage is not the answer to stemming the tide of violence in our world. As the facts show, atheists have committed far more atrocities in the world than all religious groups combined. If we would follow a biblical worldview, "Love the Lord your God with all your heart and with all your soul and with all your mind," and "Love your neighbor as yourself," this world would be transformed.

When people ask you about atrocities committed in the name of Christ, it's important to point out that those who have acted this way are following not a biblical worldview, but a sinful desire to have power over others. But don't just repeat the cliché, "Christians aren't perfect, just forgiven." It may be true, but unbelievers find it irritating. Never defend Christians who are acting sinfully.

Here are three reasons that some who claim to be Christians may act outside of a Christian worldview:
1. They are following their sinful nature.
2. They are immature in Christ. Christians are all on a spiritual journey. Some may be farther along than others. When you see a

> **totalitarian regime:** a centralized government that does not tolerate parties with differing opinions
>
> **authoritarian regime:** a political system in which the state is all powerful without protection for individual freedom, led by one or a small group of leaders not accountable to the people.

Christian, you are seeing one individual on a quest for maturity in Christ. That quest takes a lifetime, and along the way we often do fall short. That's why someone as mature as Paul says, "Follow my example as I follow the example of Christ." He is confident in his spiritual maturity and more closely reflects the character of Christ.
3. They are false believers. Not everyone who claims to be a Christian is a disciple of Jesus Christ. How can we tell if someone is a true believer? We look for the qualities that Jesus cultivates in the lives of those who belong to him. "The fruit of the Spirit," Paul tells us in Galatians 5:22-23, "is love, joy, peace, forbearance, kindness, goodness, faithfulness, gentleness and self-control. Against such things there is no law."

We must each look into our heart to see where we stand spiritually. Everyone around you may be a Christian, and you may have grown up in the church, but growing up in a church doesn't make you a Christian any more than growing up in a barn makes you a cow.

The Bible tells us to test ourselves to see if we are in Christ: "Don't you know that he is in you, unless, of course, you fail the test?" (2Cor. 13:5). Jesus called his disciples to be humble, loving, kind, compassionate and honest, and he set the example for believers to follow. The apostle John makes it very clear:

> We know that we have come to know him if we obey his commands. The man who says, 'I know him,' but does not do what he commands is a liar, and the truth is not in him. But if anyone obeys his word, God's love is truly made complete in him. This is how we know we are in him: Whoever claims to live in him must walk as Jesus did.
>
> - I John 2:3-6

A true believer will try to the best of his ability to follow the example of Jesus.

6/ Can you prove God?

PROBABLY the word that best describes my feelings about the topic of atrocities in the name of God is *frustration*, because some of it is true. It's hard to forget Jim Jones. If you're younger, Jim Jones's atrocities are where we get the phrase, "Drinking the Kool-Aid." I struggle with any form of spiritual abuse, and I've been around long enough to see some firsthand. But we live in a sinful world, and as long as there are people there will be abuse of power. The church is not exempt. The other reason the topic causes me frustration is that some of what is taught in our university classes or propagated in the media is just not true. When talking with Emily I tried not to defend the indefensible, but at the same time it's important not to go along with the cultural narrative just because you're not willing to do a little research or you're intimidated. In the end I can't change the past or control other people's hurtful behavior. All I can do—all any of us can do—is reflect God's love through our own lives. I hope that's what I'm doing with Emily.

Emily

August 2

About the beginning of the universe: I have another imagination game for you. What if I don't care how it began? What if I told you IT DOESN'T MATTER how it began? Yes, I'm yelling.

The compulsion to answer the question of where we came from (and its companion question, where we're going) has been the bane of humanity. We have invented religion, wars, fictions, rules, conflicts, and explanations *ad nauseam*.

Imagine for a moment, if you can, that it doesn't matter. Imagine if being here, presently, fully engaged in life is ALL that matters. How would that make you feel, and think?

It makes me feel free, and happy.

Jeff Greer

August 2

I've thought about it already, before I was a Christian and after. I can't just turn off my mind and enjoy "what is" because "what is" causes the questions in the first place.

Emily

August 3

I cannot, and therefore will not, accept the idea of creation. It requires me to eliminate rationality, logic, evidence—just can't do that. And I recognize how you MUST believe the creation story, for your faith rests upon it.

This is not to say I cannot believe in God, it's that I can't believe in your version of God as the creator.

Jeff Greer

August 3

Do you really believe that I am irrational, illogical and have no evidence for what I believe? Where does that leave me? Your disbelief leads you to that conclusion. I understand that. I hope I can change your perspective over time. I have not eliminated rationality, logic or evidence from my worldview.

The creation story is very important to my theological and practical understanding of the world. I agree that it is part of my foundation, but just as important is the cross and resurrection of Jesus. If Jesus was not raised from the dead, then the rest DOES NOT MATTER. I'm not sure if you understand that, so I wanted to make it clear. If you want to bring out the big guns on my worldview, that would be my true stronghold.

When you say you can believe in God, then the next question is *who is God?* What I have a difficult time understanding is if you believe in an unexplainable universe, and that luck is responsible for everything, why is it so hard to believe that God is the first cause and that he is involved in human history? You see it as illogical to believe in the Bible, but you believe the impossible in other areas.

Emily

August 3

Do I think belief in Creationism (literal understanding of Genesis, rejection of Darwin, etc.) makes you illogical? Why, YES! Yes, I do. And this is why:

God is not a scientific explanation of anything. Let me explain:

I am not an atheist, because I believe in the IDEA of god. Beautiful, powerful figment of our beautiful, powerful imagination. God moves mountains, saves souls, gives peace, implores the best of us.

But the idea of god does not speak to physics, or metaphysics, or evolution, or astrology, *et al*. God is as empirically "testable" as willpower, or love, or joy or fear.

God, or not-god, also does not explain—nor can it, in any reasonable way—disease, war, poverty, or disaster. Science explains it pretty well. Sometimes, as you point out, POLITICAL science explains it, too.

Nothing more. No greater plans (how could there be?) No punishment (How could there be that, either?) No saving, no sacrifice. No complicated books, words, miracles, rules, angels. It's

> **Creationism:** The belief that matter and everything in the universe was purposely created by God and did not arise by evolution or chance

just us. We're here and that's beautiful. We need to make the best of it. Cherish every precious minute and aspire, aspire to F L O W.

Jeff Greer

August 5

Emily, let me share a couple of other things that are not empirically testable: the origin of life, and the beginning of the universe.

How can you observe something that has already passed and draw conclusions with absolute certainty? You will never be able to create the same environment in a lab for your experiment, and if you tried you would be relying on theory to guide your decisions.

My other concern with using only empirical testing to determine truth and reality is the lost conviction that the process should be objective to avoid a biased interpretation of the results. If someone does not believe in God it is very difficult for that person to come to any conclusion that is *not* biased. All data gathered would be seen through the lens of their own worldview and presupposition. If God is "not possible," then the interpretation of all data moves in one direction.

So if scientists conclude there is no God because they will only accept proof that can be seen and measured, they have proven nothing.

Emily

August 5

I think most honest people would recognize that science has limits. When it comes to a discussion of God's existence I don't believe that you can limit your thoughts about him to empirical testing. The science of empirical testing focuses its attention on sensory perception, but I agree that there is truth beyond what we can see, touch and measure in a lab. I don't believe all truth and knowledge is limited to what can be discovered by experimentation.

 **Jeff Greer**
August 5

Let me also point out that I do not believe that science disproves in any way the existence of God. Often science is portrayed as being opposed to God, but this is untrue. As a matter of fact, science points to the existence of a God on so many levels.

I think it's presumptuous for anyone to think that they own the patent on science. It's fine to sit in a lab and try to find solutions to complex problems through empirical testing. I think it's great to try to use your senses to interpret information; we all do that. But empirical science cannot make absolute statements like, "This or that thing does not exist because I can't see it or touch it."

The finite minds and human limitations of scientists cannot understand all the realities hidden in the complexities of the universe. Emily, let's be honest—we can't even discover the true nature of matter.

Some of the examples you gave of realities that cannot be tested in the lab are what make us truly human. I also believe I can legitimately test them in the laboratory of everyday life and prove they exist.

Emily, broken bones are empirically testable, but some things that are real are not, such as love, fear, joy—and I would argue these demonstrate the existence of God.

For example, I think you have a rational, logical mind, but we cannot empirically verify that mind. We can only see the effects of your mind as they are played out in your excellent questions. In the same way, we can believe in the existence of the invisible God because of his effect in the universe and in our lives.

I have to ask: If pain, like fear and God, is not empirically testable, then why ask questions like "If there is a loving God why is there pain in the world?" According to some, to have a rational conversation on the subject of pain and suffering we would first have to empirically verify the reality of love, God, and pain. If they don't exist, why ask the question?

Do you believe in love? The Bible describes it for us:

> Love is patient, love is kind. It does not envy, it does not boast, it is not proud. It is not rude, it is not self-seeking, it is not easily angered, it keeps no record of wrongs. Love does not delight in evil but rejoices with the truth. It always protects, always trusts, always hopes, always perseveres. (I Cor. 13:4-7)

We also learn how to recognize love from biblical truth:

> This is how we know what love is: Jesus Christ laid down his life for us. And we ought to lay down our lives for our brothers. If anyone has material possessions and sees his brother in need but has no pity on him, how can the love of God be in him? Dear children, let us not love with words or tongue but with actions and in truth. (I John 3:16-18)

How can skeptics truly embrace the power of love when they're limited to live in the world of "what" and "how," while it is the "why" that gives love its meaning?

In his book *Can Man Live Without God*, Ravi Zacharias writes, "The 'what' gives us the stuff of existence; it is the 'why' that provides the glue to all that we live for and the larger interpretation of why we are here in the first place." I guess you could say that the empirically untestable—God—gives meaning to everything else that is meaningful in our lives.

My love for my family is more than a chemical reaction in my brain. I know this because I can still love when I don't feel like it. I can still be patient, kind, not envious, not boastful, not proud, not rude, not self-seeking, not easily angered, and keep no record of wrongs. I can still not delight in evil but rejoice with the truth. I can still protect, trust, hope, and persevere, even if those chemicals are not released.

I am more than the chemical and physical makeup of my parts. When my emotions or chemical reactions tell me to do one thing, I can choose to do another. My decisions defy scientific explanation.

James tells believers, "Consider it pure joy, my brothers and sisters, whenever you face trials of many kinds" (James 1:2). *What?* With trouble swirling around us, we can be joyful? Paul was, as he describes in 2 Corinthians 7:4: "I am greatly encouraged; in all our troubles my joy knows no bounds." There is something beyond chemical reactions in the brain here.

Not only are love, pain and joy real, but all of these find their purpose and value in God. When you only look at what is scientifically observable, when you eliminate God from the equation, you eliminate life's wonders—what makes us human.

I'm always amazed at what Paul calls "the peace which surpasses all understanding" (Philippians 4:7) when I see someone who has lost a spouse, or a child, or someone very close to them. I'm thinking I could never stand up under that kind of agony and grief and pain; this person must be an emotional wreck. And I would be right, from a human standpoint. But then something miraculous happens—that person receives the peace that surpasses all understanding. In the midst of terrible suffering, I can have joy. It goes beyond logical explanation. There is a God.

Emily
August 7

Sensory empiricism is not the ideal measure of concepts or ideas like love, fear—or GOD. That is exactly my point!

And likewise the contrary: love, fear and GOD are not explanations for the empirical.

While there is a whole science behind assessing something like love or fear (involving, but not limited to chemical and hormonal triggers, brain function, past psychological experience, language, culture, sociology, etc., etc.) I think most people believe that traditional empirical science is not a satisfactory tool for qualification. Or at least we don't *want* to believe that our ideas or emotions can be qualified in these terms.

We are an egotistical lot, indeed.

I AGREE that there is an ineffable nature to many of these subjects, but I'm not willing to "fill in the gaps" with God. Some people do. Makes no difference to me and I am without judgment there. But when the gap-filler takes on the role to justify, disqualify, or otherwise take the place of what truly SHOULD be left to science, that's where I'll start throwing out words like ignorance (re: evolution) and intolerance (re: non-Christians, or non-believers).

"Why not God?" is a weak argument at best. We don't say, "why not purple aliens?" and then believe in purple aliens. Well, some people do, and then we call them crazy.

Again and again, I will refer to the sage quote by Doug Adams that is on my Facebook profile: "Isn't it enough to see that a garden is beautiful without having to believe that there are fairies at the bottom of it too?"

 **Jeff Greer**
August 8

I would agree if I asked the question "Why not God?" and left it there. But Emily, I asked the question within the context of our discussion: Is love real? Yes. Is joy real? Yes. Is fear real? Yes. Is God real? Based on the evidence I would come to the same rational and logical conclusion: yes.

Also, God is the explanation for other scientific discoveries. Science uses natural laws as a guideline. Where do those laws originate? I would say with God, and so would Einstein; he called the creator a superior spirit. He said, "Everyone who is seriously engaged in the pursuit of science becomes convinced that laws of nature manifest the existence of a spirit vastly superior to that of men, and one in the face of which we with our modest powers must feel humble."

> **Albert Einstein:** German physicist and later a U.S. citizen who formulated the theory of relativity

More from Jeff

Science is not something Christians need to fear. If we truly examine it with an open mind, *science will point to the existence of God.*

God *does* speak to physics, and metaphysics, and astronomy. God speaks to all the different areas of science; he is not "outside" of science. Emily believes God is not the explanation for anything scientific, but he is the explanation for *everything* scientific.

The day after Christmas in 2014, the *Wall Street Journal* ran a remarkable article on its Opinion page, an article that became the most-read online article ever in the history of the newspaper. "Science Increasingly Makes the Case for God," by best-selling author Eric Metaxas, begins:

> In 1966 Time magazine ran a cover story asking: Is God Dead? Many have accepted the cultural narrative that he's obsolete—that as science progresses, there is less need for a "God" to explain the universe. Yet it turns out that the rumors of God's death were premature. More amazing is that the relatively recent case for his existence comes from a surprising place—science itself.

The article then tells the story of science's search for life on planets beyond our own, a search that led to the discovery that the conditions necessary for life are so fine-tuned they make not only the odds of extra-terrestrial life almost nonexistent, but the existence of our own life here on Earth, as well as the existence of the universe itself, "simply astonishing."

Metaxas says that these discoveries made in the years since 1966, when many believed science had made God obsolete, have challenged astronomers like Fred Hoyle, who coined the term Big Bang. Hoyle said his atheism was "greatly shaken," and that "a common-sense

> **Big Bang:** The theory that the expanding universe resulted from an explosion of an extremely small, hot, and dense body of matter between 12 and 20 billion years ago

interpretation of the facts suggests that a super-intellect has monkeyed with the physics, as well as with chemistry and biology." He concludes, "The numbers one calculates from the facts seem to me so overwhelming as to put this conclusion almost beyond question."

For the whole story, please read Metaxas's full article in the Resources section at the end of this book.

Despite what many people believe, science and faith are not enemies. Many scientists not only believe in God, but find science enhances their faith. Geneticist Ruth Bancewicz, author of the 2015 book *God in the Lab*, says, "What I see using the tools of biology is a world that is incredibly complex, interconnected, and very beautiful. What a great God!"[1]

7 / Pure luck or divine intervention?

AT the end of my last post I started to think a lot about the Christians I know. Over the years I've come to realize it's not the validity of the arguments that causes people to shrink back from debate, but intimidation. It's hard to think on your feet sometimes. I'll watch Ravi answer questions on YouTube and often think, "Oh man, what's he going to say in response to *that*?" It's not always the questions asked, but the arrogant and disrespectful way the questions are delivered. But Ravi always keeps his composure and answers the questions with compassion and respect.

In my case, sometimes when Emily asks a question or makes a statement, at first I'm taken aback or stumped. But, to be honest, I love her bluntness. I have come to realize that my finite mind doesn't have all the answers to these important and emotionally charged questions. I just do my best to answer each question with honesty and humility. Throughout our discussion, I've been glad to have the time to process my thoughts and consider the words I use to respond. I find myself laughing when I think about how some of these conversations might have gone if we were face to face and not on Facebook.

Emily
August 12

I know you're in the trenches and have experienced more joy and sorrow than I will ever know. I commend you for your kindness and sacrifice. Seems to me that it doesn't matter whether you draw your strength from God, or Darwin, or Elvis—as long as you are fighting injustice and doing no harm, I'M SMILING WITH YOU!

Jeff Greer

August 13

I do believe where we draw our strength from makes a difference. Darwin is dead, Elvis is dead—but Jesus is alive. I draw my strength from the power of his resurrection. The work I do is not only inspired by God, but also accomplished through his power.

For example, we just purchased a house for AIDS orphans in Nigeria. Time was running out and we were short $28,000. I didn't panic; I just prayed. The dollar to Nigerian *naira* increased from 117 to 173—that means my money was now worth almost 50% more. A group of junior high students decided to give money to the project, and someone else "felt led" to give the rest. Now in two weeks children who once had nothing will be living in one of the most amazing places you have ever seen.

You can say it was luck, but when it happens to you all the time luck or chance becomes a foolish thought. I could tell you stories that would blow your mind—really. The reason I'm able to accomplish what I do is because I believe God's promises are true. Ephesians 3:20 says that God can do immeasurably more than all we could ever ask or imagine. I can ask or imagine a lot, but he always outdoes me. When you've tasted the immeasurably more that God offers, you never want to go back to a mediocre life.

Darwin may inspire, but it ends there. When Jesus gives you a vision, the fun has just started and your accomplishments will not only be remembered in this life, but will echo in eternity.

Emily

August 15

That's awesome news about the AIDS home in Nigeria. Congratulations. Regarding HOW the funds came about: I think you and I will have to agree to disagree. Your worldview tells you it was divine intervention; mine says we should not confuse coincidence for fate. Good things happen ALL the time, as do bad. We ascribe meaning to them as we see fit.

Jeff Greer

August 16

After I wrote to you about the Oasis House in Nigeria, I thought through what I said and I anticipated your response. Good and bad things *do* happen all the time. You are correct that we need to be careful how and what we attribute to God. I do believe that God allows things to happen for a purpose, but I need to be careful how I communicate my position. Christians often speak of God's will when in fact they don't understand his will and are often wrong in their assumptions.

If you don't believe in God, I can understand the need to call things that happen in our lives coincidence. I see God as real and alive and see events in life as a part of God's ultimate plan. Let me share another example that changed my thinking about things always happening by chance.

When I was living in Marblehead, Massachusetts, I took a job as a youth pastor in a small church. The church didn't have many kids, so they told me to reach out to the community and build the group over time. To help me do that, I asked the students in the community what they wanted most. I had always seen them skating home from school, so I had an idea of what they would want, and I was right—they all said a skateboard park.

I had no idea how to build a skateboard park, but I felt in my heart God was calling me to step out and do it. I went to the town to see if they would give us some space in one of the parks, and to my surprise, they did. They gave us a broken-down basketball court in the worst part of the park, but it was ours. I rallied the troops and for a few weeks we cleaned up broken glass and pulled six-foot weeds.

When we got everything cleaned up, I started talking with people in the community about helping to build the ramps for the park. A contractor said he would help construct the foundation, but he needed plans. It just happened that a brother of one of the students was in town; he was from California and designed skateboard parks. We met, and I asked him to design something for us. (Keep in mind we had NO money.)

Two days later those two parts of the project collided. The skate park designer showed up with the plans, and when I opened them I almost laughed out loud. He had designed a horseshoe six feet tall, sixty feet long, and forty feet wide. I was about to explain to him our financial situation when the contractor showed up and saw that I had the plans. Thanking me, he took them and drove off before I could explain—I had no money. I wasn't really worried, though, because I knew that once he looked at the plans he would call me and say it was way too much for him to take on.

The next day I went to the park, and to my horror, the contractor had a dump truck at the site unloading tons of dirt and rock. He also had another piece of equipment shaping the pile into a horseshoe. (I refer you again to the fact that I had no money.) How was I going to get enough gravel and blacktop to cover this giant horseshoe ramp? Soon I would be the laughingstock of the town and probably lose my job.

My only hope was to talk with Lynn Sand and Stone, the largest stone and paving company on the North Shore. The problem was I didn't know anyone who worked there. As I walked home I began to ask myself, whose idea was this anyway? All I wanted was a little ramp for kids to skate on. Then I told God, "You're the one who wanted me to do this in the first place. Now what am I going to do?"

On my way into the house to tell Deb to start packing, I stopped at the mailbox. I pulled down the door, and there was a letter from—Lynn Sand and Stone. The address was mine, but the zip code was different. I opened it and read, "Dear John, thanks for your business. I hope you will enjoy these box seats to the Red Sox game."

The next day I took the tickets to the company and explained they had been delivered to my house by mistake. I just returned the tickets; I didn't ask about the gravel and blacktop. The woman at the reception desk took my name, thanked me, and I left.

The next day I returned to the company to talk with a different person about the skateboard park situation. He was nearly ignoring me until his secretary—the woman I had talked with the day before—told him I was the person who returned the tickets.

His attitude toward me changed immediately. It turned out this was the man who had sent them out, and he explained the tickets were for an important client, and he would have been up a creek if I had not brought them back.

"What can I do for you?" he asked. "What were you saying about blacktop and gravel?"

I explained, and he sent me to another building downtown.

I walked into the largest office I had ever seen—it belonged to the company president. He asked me how much blacktop and gravel I needed, and I said something lame like "a whole bunch." He told me to go back to the first office, and he would see what he could do. When I returned to the first office, the man there told me the president had said to give me whatever I needed.

The next day I had enough gravel and blacktop to cover the entire horseshoe. The contractor did all of his work for free, as did everyone else. It was like God said to me, "Sit down before you hurt yourself. Let me show you how to build a skate park."

God knew I needed that event to show me that he can do "immeasurably more" than I could ever imagine. And I never forgot it.

Emily, if you think that's coincidence, you have more faith in coincidence than most people have in God, and I am the luckiest person on the planet. God knew I needed that event at that time in my spiritual journey just like he knew I needed you to give me those smiley faces. You said you're not an atheist. My question is, why couldn't those events be the work of God? Why is the only option coincidence?

Emily
August 17

That's a great story. Very, very cool. And yes, you guessed it: I call it luck (and the generosity of some really nice people, including you). Are you the luckiest person on the planet? Probably not. Are you the most charming? and persistent? Maybe.

If you mean to share the story as a sort of anecdotal proof of God, sorry. Fish ain't biting. If you told me, as sure as the sun rises, that every time someone was in need the same such string of events would ensue, then I'd consider it. (Tough crowd!—but we are talking God here.) Obviously, millions, billions of desperate prayers for skateboard parks, gravel, life, and yes, even Red Sox tickets, go unanswered every day.

I know, I know, it's God's PLAN, right? He chooses what's best to answer based on his plan. But why such a convoluted series of events and people? Why not just make a park available? God sure is a micro-manager!

There is proof, and there is faith.

Jeff Greer
August 17

Again I need to ask, why not God? If a person can believe that everything can be created from nothing, why is it so impossible to believe that God intervenes in our lives? Just the fact that we exist at all is mathematically impossible, yet here we are. So why not God?

Nice people do nice things all the time, but the story wasn't about the people involved; it was about the circumstances. The moment I needed the gravel and blacktop, the tickets were in the mailbox—not a week or a month later. I didn't go up and ask the nice people and it all worked out. As a matter of fact, I wasn't even praying for it. I was complaining about it. I wasn't charming or persuasive—thank you for that—I was just along for the ride.

To understand God's plan, you need to understand God. I think part of the disconnect for you is that you don't understand God, and you sometimes seem angry with him. I hope that during our discussions I can clarify some of your questions and concerns.

Why didn't God just make a park available? He did, in an amazing way. The story was picked up by a local newspaper, and then was even on TV. Many people were completely amazed by the series of events—both Christians and non-Christians.

And because of that event my trust, faith and confidence in God grew. Belief is not easy. There are times when I call out to God and he doesn't come to my rescue or give me what I think I need. It's during those times that I remember how God has worked in the past and I draw on my faith and confidence in him.

Why don't you always give your kids what they want when they want it? Why do you discipline them? Sometimes you intervene in their lives for their benefit, and sometimes you let them fail and not intervene, hoping they will learn from the experience. Do you ever make plans and hope they will follow for their benefit, because you know best?

If you do these things as a parent, why is it so impossible to believe that a God with an infinite mind has a plan that you with your finite mind cannot comprehend? I have faith, yes, but my faith is based on evidence and experience. I don't make everything fit into a nice neat box. I ask more questions than most people ever consider. The difference is I keep asking, I keep searching, and I keep studying until I get an answer or, like everyone on the planet, I realize that some things are beyond my comprehension.

Deuteronomy 29:29 says, "The secret things are hidden with the Lord our God, but the things revealed belong to us and our children." I will never have all the answers, but I will have enough to be confident in God. (By the way, if I *did* have all the answers, everyone would worship me!) Just because we can't understand or explain something doesn't mean it isn't real.

How did the universe come into existence? How did life come about on this planet? Were any of us there? How can we really know? Whether you believe the first cause was God, or if it was nothing, it all comes down to faith. And if you believe that nothing created everything, you have more faith than I do.

You can't tell me how the universe began, but it doesn't stop you from believing that it had a beginning. You have no idea that the next chair that you sit in will hold you without breaking, yet you have faith that it will. You don't give it a moment of thought—why? There is proof and there is faith, and you have no proof that that particular chair will hold.

You're right; I can't prove that God exists. That's why Jesus said, "Blessed are they who don't see yet still believe." I believe because I've looked at the evidence and have come to the reasonable, rational and logical conclusion that God exists. I took no blind leap of faith. I stepped out in faith based on the evidence.

I have come to realize that most people who struggle with belief in God do so not because they have studied the evidence and found it wanting, but because if God does exist, they have a responsibility to that God. I was talking with a doctor I know very well, and I asked him why he did not believe in God. He said, "I don't want there to be a God, because if there is I would have to do what he says—and I don't want to have to be responsible to any god." At least he was honest.

Emily
August 19

I totally disagree with your assessment (at least for me). I DON'T struggle! Imagine, if you can, that peace and comfort that you find in your faith is the same for me in my non-faith.

Pausing while you imagine that.

I don't disbelieve because it's inconvenient, or I'm not up for the responsibility. I don't believe because it doesn't make any sense. It's not true. It's askew, convoluted, bewildering.

The elaborate concoction of tales and rules to support the belief is maddening. So, I guess yes, sometimes I may sound angry—well, more frustrated. But not with God. How could I be mad at something I don't believe in?

My chair is sturdy because physics and observation tell me it is. If I sit and fall, then science will explain why: a broken screw, a crack in the wood, I'm too fat.

My question to you is this: Why can't your acceptance of an unexplainable God be on the same footing as my acceptance of the unexplainable nothing? Granted, it's much easier to be a nonbeliever. In fact, I confess that it is downright lazy. I don't worry about sin, or heaven, or fear of judgment. On the contrary, your feeling of purpose has been the cause of countless acts of kindness and love. It's beyond commendable. An ounce of action is worth a ton of theory.

Jeff Greer

August 20

Let me share a few thoughts. First, the unexplainable nothing has no answers to our most profound human questions. Instead many of those who hold that position deflect their lack of answers by using a moral argument against God's existence. Like we discussed earlier, a common argument would be, "Why does God allow pain and suffering?"

Emily, have you ever wondered why people talk about pain and suffering the way they do? People don't just intellectually or philosophically discuss the question of pain, they put it a moral context. They use words like *unjust*. Why?

Is it not a glaring contradiction when an atheist raises the question of pain in a moral context? How can someone deny the existence of God and at the same time pose the question of pain and suffering in a moral context? Think about it. If this is not a moral universe, created by God, why pose the question morally?

When atheists present the question morally their own words build the case for belief in God. As a believer I can live out my worldview without contradiction. The same cannot be said for those who believe in the "unexplainable nothing."

As soon as they raise the question of pain and suffering in a moral context, they need to deal with their own morality. But that is in direct conflict with their stated amoral worldview.

Those who claim that God is the first cause must face the gauntlet of life-defining questions. For me, it's a never-ending search for understanding in the context of truth. Why don't we give the same scrutiny to the thinking that directs a life without God? Why are we even discussing pain and suffering in a purely materialistic, godless, unexplainable universe? Again, where is atheism when it hurts?

The unexplainable nothing offers just that—NOTHING!

The idea of an unexplainable nothing being on equal footing with God is, in my mind, flawed, to say the least. This idea popularized by the New Atheists (which is just logical positivism repackaged) fails on so many levels, and those who hold this view refuse to engage in any honest debate. They cite their lack of engagement as intellectual integrity, but as I state earlier in our conversations, that is just another way of saying they cannot defend their worldview, at best— or downright arrogance, at least.

I know you are a thinker, so I don't understand how you can hold a position that is so illogical and fraught with defiantly unanswered questions. Dawkins talks of the origins of life and consciousness as

> **logical positivism:** a 20th-century philosophy characterized by the view that scientific knowledge is the only kind of factual knowledge and that all traditional metaphysical doctrines are to be rejected as meaningless.

"on-off events triggered by an initial stroke of luck." That is not out of context; that is his position, and this from one of the leaders of the "Nothing" theory. Dennett, a hard-and-fast physicalist, wrote concerning origination, "And then a miracle happens." Emily, you told me that the search for God scientifically is futile, yet this type of thinking is worthy of lifelong discussion and investigation?

It's not only Christians who are open to the logic of an intelligent power as the first cause. For example, Einstein may have had distaste for organized religion, but it is well documented that he believed in a "superior mind" and a "superior reasoning power" at work in the laws of nature. Einstein specifically denied that he was either a pantheist or an atheist. That does not make him a Bible-believing follower of Jesus, but that is not my assertion. Stephen Hawking said that he did believe in God, but that after establishing the laws of nature and physics God has no control of the world. Again, I'm not claiming these men are Christians, just that they are open to the possibility (at least) that God exists. Many great scientists see a direct connection between their own work and a "superior being."

I think it's important to point out that a person's frustrations with organized religion, for whatever reason, have no bearing on the existence of God. I would never say that those who believe in the "unexplainable nothing" are not sincere in their position, but I could point out many ways in which I believe it falls short. I respect your right to believe that view, and your intellect is without question; that is why I am confused that you are so open to the concept of "Nothing" and so closed to the concept of God as first cause.

> **Dan Dennett:** A New Atheist philosopher who believes that human consciousness and free will are the result of physical processes in the brain and that morality and religious thought came about through evolution.
>
> **physicalist:** a follower of logical positivism, who believes that a statement is meaningful only if it refers to properties of things observable in time and space.
>
> **pantheist:** someone who believes that God is identical with the material universe or the forces of nature, that God is everything and everyone and that everyone and everything is God

More from Jeff

Is everything in life pure luck, or is God involved in helping direct our everyday lives?

No matter what I share, no matter how compelling my stories, in the end it all comes down to faith. Keep in mind our definition of faith: "Now faith is being sure of what we hope for and certain of what we do not see" (Hebrews 11:1). We are *sure*. We are *certain*.

When I was nineteen years old in New York I had just become a Christian. Every summer for six to eight years I had been getting cluster headaches. They were so bad that my eyes would swell shut, I would throw up, and the pounding pain was agonizing. Every May I would go to the doctor to get my headache medicine. When a headache came, I would take the medicine, go to a dark room, and try to go to sleep to get rid of the brutal headache. I had been a Christian for about a year, and was growing in my faith, so that year I decided I would have faith that God would heal me of these cluster headaches. I prayed, "God, I know that you can heal me if you want to. To show my faith, I'm not going to go to the doctor this year for medicine." May came; no doctor visit. June rolled by, and then July. The entire summer passed, and I never got a headache—not even a small one. I haven't had a cluster headache since then.

I was young in my faith, and my prayer was a prayer of faith. One thing I've seen as a Christian is that when we're young in our Christian walk God often answers our prayers in miraculous ways to build our faith. He intervenes because as we grow there will be seasons when we'll feel alone, and it's during those times that we need to recall the miracles of the past.

Consider this: Would it be realistic for God to say yes to everything people ask for? In the movie *Bruce Almighty*, Bruce gets to be God for a few days. People start asking him for things, and as he gets flooded with requests, he keeps pounding out "yes, yes, yes" on the computer. What happened after he said "yes" to everything? Bedlam.

There are biblical principles that help us understand why God often responds the way he does to our prayers. The timing may not be right, they are not aligned with God's will, he wants to protect us from our own destructive desires, or we have selfish motives. James 4:3 says, "When you ask, you do not receive, because you ask with wrong motives, that you may spend what you get on your pleasures." Think of the people who win the lottery and ruin their lives. What we want is not always what we need; sometimes it takes life's challenges to bring us closer to God.

We need to trust that God understands us better than we understand ourselves, and he knows what's best for us. Again, that takes faith. I have faith that there is a God with an infinite mind who knows more than I do and understands what's best for me with my finite mind.

We need to have an eternal perspective if we truly want to understand God's will and purpose. We will never have all the answers to many of life's most challenging questions, but in the end I would rather trust that when we leave this life those answers will be revealed than live in the emptiness of a world void of grace, purpose, meaning and justice.

In the end, it's our choice what to believe, but each of us needs to consider the implications of our choice:

> If it's all pure luck there is no purpose in our experiences.
> If it's all pure luck there is no hope.
> If it's all pure luck we're all in this together—alone.
> If it's all pure luck, this life is a cruel joke.
> If it's all pure luck there is no future justice.

The idea that everything is pure luck is horrifying to a world of people conscious of what is going on around them. To believe that we evolved and then were left alone to suffer makes our existence an inescapable nightmare.

Without God, the atheist Bertram Russell's summation of life was right: "Only on the firm foundation of unyielding despair can the soul's habitation be safely built." He also wrote, "Brief and powerless is Man's life; on him and all his race the slow, sure doom falls pitiless and dark."

I may not have complete answers for why things happen, but I'm confident that God will never leave me nor forsake me, and because of that I can have hope in this life and in the next.

8/ still smiling

AS I processed through my last discussion with Emily I wondered if I was making a positive impact. Then I recalled the many conversations about faith I had with family and friends early in my walk with Christ. I often wondered if they would ever open their hearts to God. I think I spent as much time praying for them as I did talking with them. My reflection on this reminded me that spiritual transformation in another person's life is not my responsibility. My job is to be faithful in sharing truth and loving others. It's the Holy Spirit's job to move their heart. I always keep in mind that God loves people more than I ever could, and it's his desire that no one would perish but all would come to repentance (2 Peter 3:9). It gives me comfort to know that I can rest in his promises and power to change lives.

Emily

April 12

Hey Jeff. Just got home a couple of hours ago from Florida. We had to get up at 3:30 a.m. to catch our flight—ARGH! You're so good to write during my time away. We had a great, great time and I thought of you quite often. Here's why:

1. First day at Epcot: airplane writer up in the bright blue sky...Was it a marriage proposal? An advertisement? NO! It read:

<big>U + God = ☺</big>

2. We saw oh, about a MILLION Christian youth groups with matching t-shirts on spring break. Everywhere!

3. We only had one sit-down meal—at a restaurant in Magic Kingdom and our server, Heidi, was a student at Liberty University. My niece, whose family prays for us all the time, is starting school there in the fall.

4. Last night, on our way out of Disney, we stopped to get souvenirs for the kids. We often look for things with their names. We can never find Jackson, but usually Jack. We rarely find Jillian, but usually Jill. Calvin—forget about it. So last night on the Mickey Mouse key chain rack: No Calvin, No Jackson OR Jack, No Jillian OR Jill, but guess what they did have in the "J" section? Yup! "Jesus"!

I thought that was pretty funny and that you would think so too. My kids said, "Get it for Jeff!" I thought you must already have one.

I can't believe that your week was so busy and you still made five entries! My goodness. I do have some catching up to do. But first I need to catch up on some sleep so I can be clear-headed.

BTW, whenever—I'd love to hear about all your S.S.F. [Superhuman Sky Fairy] lucky-duck happenings. You know how I love a good coincidence!

Zzzzzzzzz

 **Jeff Greer**
April 13

That sky writing story is amazing...did you hear the Twilight Zone music playing in your head when you saw that?

 **Emily**
April 13

No Twilight Zone music—but it did cross my mind that in your spare time you had taken up flying and made a beeline down to Florida—Ha!

Thinking the pilot would have been doing that with or without my witness. He's probably doing it right now.

More from Jeff

I can't believe the "God + U = ☺" skywriting didn't change her mind! (And after I paid all that money—just kidding!) It was the foundation of our first conversation; the gesture that started it all and the event that helped change my life. It got me thinking in ways that opened my mind to new possibilities, and ultimately it helped me discover truth. One thing I've learned over the years is that changing someone's worldview is often a process. But God is patient and so am I. Life is filled with seasons, experiences, and opportunities, and if you love people you can't force change. So I guess this part of the story is going to end like the season finale of many of our favorite TV shows: To Be Continued...

Some final thoughts

I had been a Christian only about six months when I started Bible college. During the summer after my freshman year, I took a history course I needed at a state university. Very quickly I learned that the professor hated two groups of people: women and Christians. I think he hated Christians more. Throughout his lectures, he would ridicule women and criticize Christians. He believed Christians were responsible for every ill that ever happened in society. The professor would smoke during class (that was okay back in those days), and he used a church offering plate as an ashtray. In a desire to defend my faith, I would question some of the things the professor said, so he quickly realized I was a Christian, and I became the target for his persecution. Being a new Christian, I didn't know very much, so I would just make comments like, "That's a fact, correct?"

When I finally drove him nuts, he stopped the class. "Listen to me," he yelled, writing on the blackboard. "Your truth is your truth because you believe it, and my truth is my truth because I believe it." He then spent about twenty minutes explaining "truth" to me.

When he was finished, I told him, "But I'm not in class presenting my truth as fact; you are. I'm a student asking a question. I just want to know if what you're saying *is* a fact, because you're going to be testing me on it." He said something to keep me quiet and went on with his lecture.

After that episode, I began sitting in the front row of the class, smiling and wearing a big button that said "Jesus Loves You." I didn't know how to refute what he was teaching so that's all I could do.

If you happen to be headed to college, know that your faith is going to be challenged. If you stand up for yourself, the professors will try to mow you over—they know you're young and not used to this kind of debate, and they've had students like you for years. Most professors don't want you to ask the questions, because they don't want to engage in an intellectual conversation. They have no desire to help you work through what you believe and why. Instead, they will often attempt to push their worldview by belittling you or using verbal intimidation. Christians are not to be afraid of what men can do to them. Look at Matthew 10:28: "Do not be afraid of those who kill the body but cannot kill the soul. Rather, be afraid of the One who can destroy both soul and body in hell." Matthew is saying we are to fear God rather than men. Remember this when you're in class or at work defending your faith.

Our world is full of skeptics and so much demonic activity it's a guarantee that you will be persecuted; that is, if you are living for Christ. If you are never persecuted for your faith, then you're probably not making any noise. This doesn't mean that if you are not persecuted you're not a good Christian. But it does mean that the gospel sometimes offends people and you can suffer the consequences. It's important to be in right standing with God so when you are slandered, the accusation will have no basis in truth and you can easily defend your position. Sometimes you will suffer for doing what's right. Sometimes when you stand up for truth, you will be unjustly accused. But in those times, you should be so centered on Jesus, so close to him, so sure of him, that when you're persecuted you have no fear.

The way you overcome the fear of sharing is by putting Christ first in your life and by living out what you say you believe with boldness. The Bible says, "Stand strong; let nothing move you!" That is my encouragement to you. Go speak the truth, go live the truth!

Notes

[1] "God in the Lab: how science enhances faith, and vice versa," *Christianity Today*, 15 Feb. 2015.
<http://www.christiantoday.com/article/god.in.the.lab.how.science.enhances.faith.and.vice.versa/47995.htm>

Resources

Table 1: Pre-20th Century Democide

Table 2: 20th Century Democide

What's the Truth about the Crusades?

Article: "Science Increasingly Makes the Case for God"

Suggestions for Further Study: Web and Print Resources

Glossary

TABLE 1. Democide (murder by government) in thousands

Selected Pre-20th Century Democide and Totals [1]

Cases	Years [2]	Democide (000) [3]	
In China	221 B.C.-19 C. A.D.	33,519	[4]
By Mongols	14 C-15 C	29,927	
Slavery of Africans	1451-1870	17,267	
Of Amer-Indians	16 C-19 C	13,778	
Thirty Years War	1618-1648	5,750	
In India	13 C-19 C	4,511	[5]
In Iran	5 C-19 C	2,000	[4,5]
In Ottoman Empire	12 C-19 C	2,000	[5]
In Japan	1570-19 C	1,500	[5]
In Russia	10 C-19 C	1,007	[5]
Christian Crusades	1095-1272	1,000	
By Aztecs	Centuries	1,000	[6]
Spanish Inquisition	16 C-18 C	350	
French Revolution	1793-1794	263	
Albigensian Crusade	1208-1249	200	
Witch Hunts	15 C-17 C	100	
Total For All Cases	pre-20 C	133,147	
Hypothetical Total	30C B.C.-19C A.D.	625,716	[7]
Inter'l war-related dead	30C B.C.-19C A.D.	40,457	[8]
Plague dead (Black Death)	541 A.D.-1912	102,070	[9]

1. From STATISTICS OF DEMOCIDE.
2. Unless otherwise noted, years and centuries are A.D.
3. Unless otherwise noted, these are a best guess estimate in a low to high range
4. Excludes democide in China by Mongols.
5. An absolute low.
6. A very speculative absolute low.
7. From STATISTICS OF DEMOCIDE.. Calculated from the 20th C. democide rate and the population for each century since 30 B.C.
8. From table STATISTICS OF DEMOCIDE. Total undoubtedly inflated by democide.
9. A minimum: includes plague dead in circa 541-542 A.D.; 1346-1771 in Europe; 1771 in Moscow; 1894 in Hong Kong; and 1898-1912 in India. From Duplaix (1988, p. 677-678).

Rudolph Rummel, http://www.hawaii.edu/powerkills/murder.htm

TABLE 2. Democide (murder by government) in thousands

20th Century Democide

REGIMES	YEARS	DEMOCIDE (000)[1]			ANNUAL RATE %[2]	
		TOTAL	DOMESTIC	GENOCIDE		
MEGAMURDERERS	**1900-87**	**151,491**	**116,380**	**33,476**		**[4]**
DEKA-MEGAMURDERERS	1900-87	128,168	100,842	26,690	0.18	[4]
U.S.S.R.	1917-87	61,911	54,769	10,000	0.42	
China (PRC)	1949-87	35,236	35,236	375	0.12	
Germany	1933-45	20,946	762	16,315	0.09	
China (KMT)	1928-49	10,075	10,075	Nil	0.07	[5]
LESSER MEGAMURDERS	1900-87	19,178	12,237	6,184	1.63	[4]
Japan	1936-45	5,964	Nil	Nil	Nil	
China (Mao Soviets) [3]	1923-49	3,466	3,466	Nil	0.05	[5]
Cambodia	1975-79	2,035	2,000	541	8.16	
Turkey	1909-18	1,883	1,752	1,883	0.96	
Vietnam	1945-87	1,670	944	Nil	0.10	
Poland	1945-48	1,585	1,585	1,585	1.99	
Pakistan	1958-87	1,503	1,503	1,500	0.06	
Yugoslavia (Tito)	1944-87	1,072	987	675	0.12	
SUSPECTED MEGAMURDE	1900-87	4,145	3,301	602	0.24	[4]
North Korea	1948-87	1,663	1,293	Nil	0.25	
Mexico	1900-20	1,417	1,417	100	0.45	
Russia	1900-17	1,066	591	502	0.02	
CENTI-KILOMURDERERS	**1900-87**	**14,918**	**10,812**	**4,071**	**0.26**	**[4]**
TOP 5	1900-87	4,074	2,192	1,078	0.89	[4]
China (Warlords)	1917-49	910	910	Nil	0.02	
Turkey (Atatürk)	1919-23	878	703	878	2.64	
United Kingdom	1900-87	816	Nil	Nil	Nil	
Portugal (Dictatorship)	1926-82	741	Nil	Nil	Nil	
Indonesia	1965-87	729	579	200	0.02	
LESSER MURDERERS	**1900-87**	**2,792**	**2,355**	**1,019**	**.1**	**[4]**
WORLD TOTAL	**1900-87**	**169,202**	**129,547**	**38,566**	**.1**	**[6]**

1. Includes genocide, politicide, and mass murder; excludes war-dead.
   These are most probable mid-estimates in low to high ranges.
   Figures may not sum due to round off.
2. The percent of a population killed in democide per year of the regime
3. Guerrilla period. 4. Average.
5. The rate is the average of that for three successive periods.
6. The world annual rate is calculated for the 1944 global population

Rudolph Rummel, <http://www.hawaii.edu/powerkills/murder.htm>

What's the Truth about the Crusades?

Within a month of the 9/11 attacks, in a speech at Georgetown University, former president Bill Clinton said the Crusades were the root cause of Islamic terrorism and our modern-day conflicts. Clinton remarked that "when the Christian soldiers took Jerusalem [in 1099], they . . . proceeded to kill every woman and child who was Muslim on the Temple Mount." He said sources describe "soldiers walking on the Temple Mount . . . with blood running up to their knees." This story, Mr. Clinton said, was "still being told today in the Middle East and we are still paying for it."[1]

Bill Clinton's point makes very little sense to me, since Islamist terrorists hate the Jewish people. But it's all I've ever heard—the Crusades were the dark ages of the faith. And how could I question the History Channel or my favorite Robin Hood movie? This view of the Crusaders as violent bigots is even found in textbooks and video games.

It makes no sense. Christianity throughout history has not spread through violence, but through evangelism and even persecution. We see this with Paul in early Rome. Why would Christians change their mode of spreading the gospel? Why would they start to attack "innocent people" in an attempt to force their religion on them?

Earlier history provides insight into the Crusades. When Mohammed started waging war against Mecca in the seventh century, Christianity was the dominant religion of power and wealth. It was spread throughout the Mediterranean, which included the Middle East, its place of birth. Because of that, Christianity became the prime target of Islam and it stayed that way for a thousand years.

Muslims quickly took Palestine, Syria, and Egypt. These were once very populated Christian areas. By the eighth century, they had conquered all of Christian North Africa and Spain. The conquests continued and by the eleventh century, the Seljuk Turks conquered what is now modern Turkey. That area had been Christian since the time of Paul.

This went on until the old Roman Empire was reduced to Greece. Christianity was being crushed under the power of Islam. The emperor in Constantinople sent word to the Christians in Western Europe: their brothers and sisters in the East were being persecuted and needed help.

Pope Urban II responded by calling together French clerics and laymen to discuss the matter. The pope's message at this Council of Clermont in 1095 was moving and memorable, and it launched the first Crusade. His words that day were not recorded, but we have several accounts written by people in attendance. The details differ, but E. L. Skip Knox, a Medieval History professor at Boise State University, sums up the main message:

> *The noble race of Franks,* the pope said, *must come to the aid of their fellow Christians in the East. The infidel Turks are advancing into the heart of Eastern Christendom; Christians are being oppressed and attacked; churches and holy places are being defiled. Jerusalem is groaning under the Saracen yoke. The Holy Sepulchre is in Moslem hands and has been turned into a mosque. Pilgrims are harassed and even prevented from access to the Holy Land.*
>
> *The West must march to the defense of the East. All should go, rich and poor alike. The Franks must stop their internal wars and squabbles. Let them go instead against the infidel and fight a righteous war.*
>
> *God himself would lead them, for they would be doing His work. There will be absolution and remission of sins for all who die in the service of Christ. Here they are poor and miserable sinners; there they will be rich and happy. Let none hesitate; they must march next summer. God wills it!*[2]

In December 1095, the pope sent this letter of instruction to the Crusaders:

> Urban, bishop, servant of the servants of God, to all the faithful, both princes and subjects, waiting in Flanders; greeting, apostolic grace, and blessing.
>
> Your brotherhood, we believe, has long since learned from many accounts that a barbaric fury has deplorably afflicted and laid waste the churches of God in the regions of the Orient. More than this, blasphemous to say, it has even grasped in intolerable servitude its churches and the Holy City of Christ, glorified by His passion and resurrection. Grieving with pious

concern at this calamity, we visited the regions of Gaul and devoted ourselves largely to urging the princes of the land and their subjects to free the churches of the East. We solemnly enjoined upon them at the council of Auvergne (the accomplishment of) such an undertaking, as a preparation for the remission of all their sins. And we have constituted our most beloved son, Adhemar, Bishop of Puy, leader of this expedition and undertaking in our stead, so that those who, perchance, may wish to undertake this journey should comply with his commands, as if they were our own, and submit fully to his loosings or bindings, as far as shall seem to belong to such an office. If, moreover, there are any of your people whom God has inspired to this vow, let them know that he (Adhemar) will set out with the aid of God on the day of the Assumption of the Blessed Mary, and that they can then attach themselves to his following.

Pope Urban II's successor, Innocent III, wrote:

How does a man love according to divine precept his neighbor as himself when, knowing that his Christian brothers in faith and in name are held by the perfidious Muslims in strict confinement and weighed down by the yoke of heaviest servitude, he does not devote himself to the task of freeing them? ... Is it by chance that you do not know that many thousands of Christians are bound in slavery and imprisoned by the Muslims, tortured with innumerable torments?

These writings from the religious leaders themselves give insight into the thoughts and feelings behind the Crusades better than someone's interpretation centuries later ever could. These wars were not started to gain power or money, but to fight against more than four centuries of conquests. Muslims had taken two-thirds of the old Christian world. Christians had a choice: defend themselves or be overcome by Islam. The Crusades were seen by most of the people involved as an act of love and mercy.

I think those who believe the motive behind the Crusades was a grab for greater power by the religious leaders of the day must come to this conclusion by interjecting their own personal feelings about religion, and the Catholic Church in particular, into ancient history. I would rather just take the original writers at their word, because it's all we have.

We are also taught that the goal of the Crusades was to force Muslims to convert, but that's not true. There is no strong historical evidence to back up that claim and it is a confusing concept to anyone who understands a biblical worldview. I did read that the Franciscans tried conversion but they were for the most part unsuccessful. Regardless, their efforts were always by peaceful persuasion, not the threat of violence.

Yes, there were brutal attacks against innocent people, including the Jews. When the Second Crusade was starting up, St. Bernard wrote, "Ask anyone who knows the Sacred Scriptures what he finds foretold of the Jews in the Psalm. 'Not for their destruction do I pray,' it says. The Jews are for us the living words of Scripture, for they remind us always of what our Lord suffered ... Under Christian princes they endure a hard captivity, but 'they only wait for the time of their deliverance.'"

Even with that affirmation of Jews as a backdrop, a fellow monk named Radulf got people all fired up to attack the Rhineland Jews. Bernard did everything he could to end the attacks. He sent letter after letter demanding that Radulf stop. Bernard then took it upon himself to travel to Germany to confront Radulf. He ended up sending him back to his monastery, and ended the attacks.

In every day and age, there are people who follow their sinful nature and commit atrocious acts of violence. It happened in the Crusades, and it is inexcusable, but my point here is that the violence was not sanctioned by the Crusade movement.

The Crusades were war, and war is violent. I know people say, "How can religious people justify going to war?" But to be honest, after 9/11, the bombings around the world, the beheadings of Christians in Egypt and kidnaping of children in Africa, I'm not surprised by the European Christians' response. Remember this Muslim aggression had been going on for hundreds of years.

My study of the Crusades has made it clear that the present day challenges we face with Islam are not based on circumstances that took place 1000 years ago, but are instead rooted in the Islamic worldview. While many Muslims are peaceful, Islam was born in war and grew the same way. Starting with Mohammed, their means of expansion was violent overthrow. What I've learned is that Muslims separate the world into two camps: us and them. Christians, Jews or any other religion or people group may often be tolerated within a Muslim state, but only if they are under Muslim rule. We see that in Middle Eastern countries today. In traditional Islam, Christian and Jewish states must be conquered and their lands taken.

This makes sense to me because I was wondering why the Crusaders would have to fight for land that they had been settled in for centuries. Jews and Christians had been in those areas before Islam came into existence. So why are the Crusades seen today as an unprovoked, intolerant violent attack against Islam?

Steve Weidenkopf in his book *The Glory of the Crusades* writes, "Most people's impression of the Crusades is fostered by Hollywood movies and documentaries on TV. Although this has led to wide recognition of the subject, that presentation of the Crusades is false and greatly misleading because Hollywood and TV rely on an outdated anti-Christian narrative."

Weidenkopf goes on:

> The negative 'spin' actually began in the sixteenth century with Martin Luther, who attacked the Crusades because he saw them as an outgrowth of papal authority and power. In subsequent centuries, Enlightenment authors like Voltaire and Edward Gibbon (among others) shaped modernity's negative view of the Crusades by seeing them as barbaric events undertaken by greedy and savage warriors at the behest of a corrupt papacy.

> This anti-religious view of the inherently religious Crusades shaped popular imagination about the events. In the middle of the 20th century Sir Steven Runciman, an English historian of Byzantium, published the immensely popular three-volume

History of the Crusades. Runciman's work was more literature than history but his narrative style led to a wide audience of readers. He embraced the Enlightenment and Byzantine (Eastern) view of the Crusaders and it's this view that is portrayed in films and documentaries. Thankfully, modern-day Crusade historians eschew this prejudice and are bringing to light an authentic understanding of these important Christian events.[3]

There is so much more to the history of the Crusades, but I'll stop there. I think I've given an honest description of why I believe they took place and the steps that were taken to avoid the sometimes senseless brutality of war.

---

[1]Crawford, Paul. "Four Myths about the Crusades." The Intercollegiate Review (Spring, 2011).
http://www.mmisi.org/ir/46_01/crawford.pdf

[2]Knox, E. L. Skip, *History of the Crusades.* Boise State University.
http://europeanhistory.boisestate.edu/crusades/1st/02.shtml

[3]Weidenkopf, Steve. The Glory of the Crusades. Catholic Answers Press, 2014.

Science Increasingly Makes the Case for God

by Eric Metaxas

In 1966 Time magazine ran a cover story asking: Is God Dead? Many have accepted the cultural narrative that he's obsolete—that as science progresses, there is less need for a "God" to explain the universe. Yet it turns out that the rumors of God's death were premature. More amazing is that the relatively recent case for his existence comes from a surprising place—science itself.

Here's the story: The same year Time featured the now-famous headline, the astronomer Carl Sagan announced that there were two important criteria for a planet to support life: The right kind of star, and a planet the right distance from that star. Given the roughly octillion—1 followed by 27 zeros—planets in the universe, there should have been about septillion—1 followed by 24 zeros—planets capable of supporting life.

With such spectacular odds, the Search for Extraterrestrial Intelligence, a large, expensive collection of private and publicly funded projects launched in the 1960s, was sure to turn up something soon. Scientists listened with a vast radio telescopic network for signals that resembled coded intelligence and were not merely random. But as years passed, the silence from the rest of the universe was deafening. Congress defunded SETI in 1993, but the search continues with private funds. As of 2014, researchers have discovered precisely bubkis—0 followed by nothing.

What happened? As our knowledge of the universe increased, it became clear that there were far more factors necessary for life than Sagan supposed. His two parameters grew to 10 and then 20 and then 50, and so the number of potentially life-supporting planets decreased accordingly. The number dropped to a few thousand planets and kept on plummeting.

Even SETI proponents acknowledged the problem. Peter Schenkel wrote in a 2006 piece for Skeptical Inquirer magazine: "In light of new findings and insights, it seems appropriate to put excessive euphoria to rest . . . . We should quietly admit that the early estimates . . . may no longer be tenable."

As factors continued to be discovered, the number of possible planets hit zero, and kept going. In other words, the odds turned against any planet in the universe supporting life, including this one. Probability said that even we shouldn't be here.

Today there are more than 200 known parameters necessary for a planet to support life—every single one of which must be perfectly met, or the whole thing falls apart. Without a massive planet like Jupiter nearby, whose gravity will draw away asteroids, a thousand times as many would hit Earth's surface. The odds against life in the universe are simply astonishing.

Yet here we are, not only existing, but talking about existing. What can account for it? Can every one of those many parameters have been perfect by accident? At what point is it fair to admit that science suggests that we cannot be the result of random forces? Doesn't assuming that an intelligence created these perfect conditions require far less faith than believing that a life-sustaining Earth just happened to beat the inconceivable odds to come into being?

There's more. The fine-tuning necessary for life to exist on a planet is nothing compared with the fine-tuning required for the universe to exist at all. For example, astrophysicists now know that the values of the four fundamental forces—gravity, the electromagnetic force, and the "strong" and "weak" nuclear forces—were determined less than one millionth of a second after the big bang. Alter any one value and the universe could not exist. For instance, if the ratio between the nuclear strong force and the electromagnetic force had been off by the tiniest fraction of the tiniest fraction—by even one part in 100,000,000,000,000,000—then no stars could have ever formed at all. Feel free to gulp.

Multiply that single parameter by all the other necessary conditions, and the odds against the universe existing are so heart-stoppingly astronomical that the notion that it all "just happened" defies common sense. It would be like tossing a coin and having it come up heads 10 quintillion times in a row. Really?

Fred Hoyle, the astronomer who coined the term "big bang," said that his atheism was "greatly shaken" at these developments. He later wrote that "a common-sense interpretation of the facts suggests that a super-intellect has monkeyed with the physics, as well as with chemistry and biology . . . . The numbers one calculates from the facts seem to me so overwhelming as to put this conclusion almost beyond question."

Theoretical physicist Paul Davies has said that "the appearance of design is overwhelming" and Oxford professor Dr. John Lennox has said "the more we get to know about our universe, the more the hypothesis that there is a Creator . . . gains in credibility as the best explanation of why we are here."

The greatest miracle of all time, without any close seconds, is the universe. It is the miracle of all miracles, one that ineluctably points with the combined brightness of every star to something—or Someone—beyond itself.

Reprinted from *The Wall Street Journal* © 2014, Dow Jones & Company. All rights reserved.

Note: A Prager University video presentation of this article, entitled "Does Science Argue for or against God?" is available on YouTube:

https://www.youtube.com/watch?v=UjGPHF5A6Po

Suggestions for Further Study

Books

Geisler, Norman, and Frank Turek. *I Don't Have Enough Faith to Be an Atheist.* Crossway, 2004.

Geisler, Norman, and Ronald M. Brooks. *When Skeptics Ask.* Baker Books, 2013.

Geisler, Norman, and Thomas Howe. *When Critics Ask.* Baker Books, 1992.

Lewis, C.S. *Mere Christianity.* Adapted from a series of radio talks between 1942 and 1944. Various editions available.

McDowell, Josh, and Sean McDowell. *More Than a Carpenter.* Tyndale, 2009.

Moreland, J.P. *Scaling the Secular City.* Baker Books, 1987.

Sproul, R.C., and Keith Mathison. *Not a Chance.* Baker Books, 2014.

Strobel, Lee. *The Case for Christ.* Zondervan, 1988.

Zacharias, Ravi:

Can Man Live Without God. Thomas Nelson, 2004.

Cries of the Heart. Thomas Nelson, 2002.

Deliver Us from Evil. Thomas Nelson, 1998.

The Grand Weaver. Zondervan, 2009.

A Shattered Visage. Baker Books, 2004.

Web

Answers in Genesis
   http://www.answersingenesis.org/

Apologetics 315
   http://www.apologetics315.com/

Apologetics Press
   http://www.apologeticspress.org/

Bethinking.org
   http://www.bethinking.org/

Christian Answers Network
   http://www.christiananswers.net/

Christian Apologetics & Research Ministry
   http://www.carm.org/

Evidence for God from Science
   http://godandscience.org/

GotQuestions.org
   http://www.gotquestions.org/

InPlainSite.org
   http://www.inplainsite.org/

Investigating Faith (Lee Strobel's Official Website)
   http://www.leestrobel.com/

The One-Minute Apologist
   https://www.youtube.com/user/oneminuteapologist

Ravi Zacharias International Ministries
   http://rzim.org/

Reasonable Faith with William Lane Craig
   http://www.reasonablefaith.org/

Reasons to Believe
   http://www.reasons.org/

Stand to Reason
   http://www.str.org/

Windmill Ministries
   http://windmillministries.org/

Xenos Christian Fellowship
   http://www.xenos.org/essays/apologetics

Glossary

The following definitions reflect how the terms are used in this book, and may not include other possible meanings.

absolute
: something that does not depend on anything else for its existence or for its specific nature (opposed to relative).

agnostic
: a person who believes that knowledge of God is impossible

atheist
: a person who believes there is no God or supreme being.

authoritarian regime
: a political system in which the state is all powerful with no protection for individual freedom, led by one or a small group of leaders that is not accountable to the people.

Beatitudes
: the eight sayings of Jesus in the Sermon on the Mount that begin with the word "Blessed."

Big Bang
: the theory that the expanding universe resulted from an explosion of an extremely small, hot, and dense body of matter between 12 and 20 billion years ago

born-again Christian
: someone who has repented of their sins and turned to Christ to be saved from spiritual death, entering into a personal relationship with God.

caste system
: the rigid Hindu system of social classification passed from one generation to the next

Chesterton, G.K.
: an early 20th-century English author of hundreds of books, poems, essays, and stories

Creationism
: the belief that matter and everything in the universe was purposely created by God and did not arise by evolution or chance

Darwin, Charles
: English naturalist who formulated the theory of evolution by natural selection

Darwinist
  one who follows Charles Darwin's theory that new species arise (evolve) from earlier forms through natural selection
Dawkins, Richard
  a British biologist and atheist known for his criticism of creationism and intelligent design
Dennett, Dan
  a New Atheist philosopher who believes that human consciousness and free will are the result of physical processes in the brain and that morality and religious thought came about through evolution.
dogma
  an official system of principles and beliefs, especially in a church.
D'Souza, Dinesh
  an Indian-American political commentator, author, and defender of Christian beliefs
Einstein, Albert
  German physicist and later U.S. citizen who formulated the theory of relativity
empirical
  provable or verifiable by experience or experiment
evolution
  genetic change passed on from generation to generation by such processes as mutation, natural selection, and genetic drift. Here, it is used to mean development of one species into a different species.
Flew, Antony
  a philosopher who was an atheist most of his life but later came to believe in God based on scientific evidence.
genocide
  deliberate and systematic extermination of a national, racial or cultural group
Harris, Sam
  a critic of religion and considered the father of "New Atheism."
Hawking, Stephen
  a physicist, cosmologist, and author, widely known for his groundbreaking work despite having a severe disability.
heretic
  a person who has beliefs contrary to those taught by his or her church
Hitchens, Christopher
  an English author, religious and literary critic, known for criticizing popular religious and political figures

Immaculate Conception
: the Catholic doctrine that the Virgin Mary was conceived without any stain of original sin

imperialist
: exercising the rule or authority of an empire or nation over foreign countries

Islamic
: following the Muslim religion, founded by the prophet Muhammad and taught by the Koran; relating to the countries and cultures that follow the Muslim religion

Kant, Immanuel
: an 18th-century German philosopher who believed that the world is unknowable and morals are based on human reasoning. Considered the father of modern philosophy.

logical positivism
: a 20th-century philosophy characterized by the view that scientific knowledge is the only kind of factual knowledge and that all traditional metaphysical doctrines are to be rejected as meaningless.

Mao Zedong
: a Communist dictator who was chairman of the People's Republic of China from 1949–59. Chairman Mao was responsible for an estimated 40 to 70 million deaths through starvation, forced labor and executions of his own people

martyr
: a person who is put to death because of his or her religion

Mein Kampf
: the autobiography of Adolph Hitler that presented his philosophy and his plan for German conquest

metaphysical
: concerned with abstract thought or subjects, such as existence, causality, or truth.

moral law
: the rules of behavior a group of people follow out of conscience and that are not necessarily part of written law

moral universe
: a basically spiritual universe that is ordered by a higher power and influenced by good and evil

naturalistic worldview
: the belief that nature is the only reality, and it can be understood through experience, reason, and science

New Atheists
early 21st-century authors who share the central belief that there is no supernatural or divine reality of any kind; that religious belief is irrational and empirical science is the only or best source of knowledge; and that there is a universal and objective secular moral standard. This moral component and their more aggressive attacks on religion set them apart from Old Atheists.

Nietzsche, Friedrich
a 19th-century German philosopher who denounced religion, rejected Christian values, and advocated nihilism.

nihilist
a person who believes that truth and values are baseless, and life has no meaning or purpose.

nullifidian
a person who has no faith or religion

Old Atheists
people who adhere to the traditional belief that there is no supreme being or beings, differing from 21st-century New Atheists who are openly antagonistic to religion and whose beliefs are typically based more in science than in philosophy

omnipotent, omniscient, omnibenevolent
all-powerful, all-knowing, all-good

pagan
a person who worships nature or the earth

pantheist
someone who believes that God is identical with the material universe or the forces of nature, that God is everything and everyone and that everyone and everything is God

physicalist
a follower of logical positivism, who believes that a statement is meaningful only if it refers to properties of things observable in time and space.

Platonic
relating to the philosophy of Plato, an ancient Greek who questioned the reality of the material world

politicide
systematic destruction of a people belonging to a specific political movement

polytheistic
believing in more than one god

Rand, Ayn
a Russian-born author and philosopher who developed Objectivism, a practical philosophy that rejects faith and religion. Politically, she supported individual rights in a capitalistic system.

relative
existing or having its specific nature only by relation to something else; not absolute or independent

semantics
the study of the relationship between words or symbols and what they mean

skeptic
a person who doubts the truth of Christianity

Social Darwinism
the belief that Darwin's theory of evolution in nature also applies to society, with the best adapted individuals or societies prevailing over those that are weaker

temporal
concerned only with the present life or this world

theist
someone who believes that one god created and rules the universe

totalitarian regime
a centralized government that does not tolerate parties with differing opinions

transubstantiation
the Catholic belief that the bread and wine are changed into the body and blood of Jesus during Communion

Unitarian
a liberal denomination that believes God is one being, rejecting the doctrine of the Trinity

Voltaire
an 18th-century French philosopher who was highly critical of religion

Zacharias, Ravi
a philosopher, author, and speaker who presents logical defense for Christian beliefs and principles

www.ingramcontent.com/pod-product-compliance
Lightning Source LLC
Chambersburg PA
CBHW032042290426
44110CB00012B/916